Beyond the Open Door

The Un-Shuttable Doors at the End of the Age

Gary DePasquale

 Scripture quotations are from the New King James Version unless otherwise noted.

First Publishing 2022

Eastern Gate Publishing
Cranford, New Jersey

Cover design: Roger Davila

ISBN: 9798417682681

International House of Prayer Eastern Gate
950 Raritan Rd.
Cranford, NJ 07016
www.ihopeg.org

Printed in the United States of America

"In this unusual hour of history, there are so few resources and written works whose aim is to equip the Saints to engage with delight with the heart of the Lord. My dear friend, Gary DePasquale, has labored to produce such a resource at just the right time. Forged from the place of long-term prayer, fasting, and focused research, Gary has given us all the gift of perspective and wisdom for these uncertain times. What a light in the darkness! I thank the Lord for Gary and for this book."

-David Sliker, President of the International House of Prayer University, Kansas City, Missouri

"We've had the privilege of knowing our friend, Pastor Gary DePasquale, for over a decade in ministry. In our humble opinion he has one of the most sound revelations of the modern day church and where it fits in God's End-Time plan. *Beyond The Open Door* will fuel your passion for Jesus and add a greater depth to your prayer life. Read this book and get equipped to understand the days ahead of us as you grow deeper in love with Jesus."

-Will and Dehavilland Ford, www.818TheSign.org. Will is the author of *The Dream King: How The Dream Of Martin Luther King Jr. Is Being Fulfilled To Heal Racism In America.*

"Jesus commanded not to let the fear of trouble dominate hearts (Jn. 14:1). Fear must be resisted and diffused by embracing the truths of the Word of God. People will search in many places for answers to alleviate fear. Gary has brought about a comprehensive look into the confidence needed to help the church alleviate those fears. I've known Gary for over two decades and he walks out what he teaches. *Beyond the Open Door* is the 'real deal.'"

-Mike Bickle, Founder, International House of Prayer of Kansas City

"When I read *Beyond the Open Door*, I felt that my friend, Gary, has been compelled by the deep love of Christ in the Holy Spirit and His love for the end-times church. This book contains inspiration keys which give you understanding and courage to be fruitful in current and future uncertain times. It brings forth the Scripture vision of a victorious family of Christ amidst birth pangs and tribulations. Let this book inspire you with the compelling love of Christ."

-Daniel Lim, teacher, lecturer, author of *Bible 360*

"My friend, Gary DePasquale, has written an important book calling us to prepare for birth pangs and to prepare for the coming of the Lord. We do have victory but victory through tribulation. I trust that God will prepare you and increase your courage and resolve through this book."

-Daniel Juster, Th. D. Restoration from Zion of Tikkun Global

"Perseverance was called 'the queen of virtues' by the ancients. Persevering faith opens to us the greatest kingdom doors. Through the power of God's word, Gary's pen will inspire your resolve to endure all the way to the end. With each chapter of this book speak Jesus' words, 'See, I have set before you an open door.'"

-Bob Sorge, Author, *God's Still Writing Your Story*

"*Beyond the Open Door* is written by a true man after God's Heart who has also become my dear friend. Gary De Pasquale has heard the call, 'Church, you must awaken before it's too late!' While these ends of days will be most glorious, they will also be challenging, and we must now face these realities to get ready. This book will challenge you to greater heights in God's Kingdom and into the preparations that are now needed for God's family to walk out the days beyond the open door."

-Grant Berry, Founder Reconnecting Ministries, Author, Producer of The Romans 911 Project

Contents

DEDICATION AND ACKNOWLEDGMENTS

I would like to bring acknowledgment to a couple of people that I walked with and observed during the writing of this book. They are people that have been long in the faith that I had admired in my youth but have faced trials of some of the most difficult that people can experience and remain steadfast. I think of Bob Zebro who has been a long time personal supporter and mentor of mine since I was 13 years old. And though he is facing such a large trial he still maintains a grateful heart towards the Lord and brings glory to His name. Also, Leo and Eileen Borre who have been a constant source of stability in the ministry and more recently a picture of total dependency upon their faith in Jesus. The Grazio's who have been a model of hospitality and giving even through the season of testing and have always landed in the place of the sustainable dedication to His Word. And finally, my mother, whom I have had the honor of caring for these last twenty-four years since the passing of my dad. In these last two years she has walked through fire and still is standing with the hope of glory. There are more, but it is these I would like to acknowledge as being a source of inspiration and encouragement of persevering in the Lord.

I would like to bring dedication to the leadership staff and the missionary staff of the International House of Prayer Eastern Gate that are still showing up, still singing, still praying, and still expecting for the more of God to come. There has never been a more dedicated and faith-filled group of people that I have seen in all of my years. We are all waiting for the moment when night and day prayer rooms will not be considered a waste of time and intercessory missionaries will warrant the respect of pastors and leaders as a necessary place of end-time ministry. These people have given up money, career, position, honor, glory, and have counted it all as loss for the sake of knowing and ministering unto Jesus day and night. As long as I live and into glory this will be my honor to have known and served with a people of whom the world despises.

Specific thanks to Mike and Alicia for your editing prowess and to Roger for the eye of the Holy Spirit in creating the visual expression of this book. Without all of you this would have not come together the way that it has. You have all gone above and beyond for this message to be released to the greater body of Christ.

Unto His Return!

Gary DePasquale

FOREWORD

If we survey the New Testament to identify the most emphasized of Christian virtues, there are few that easily rise to the surface: Love, faith, hope, and humility certainly spring to mind. These are all praiseworthy character traits produced as a fruit of the Holy Spirit's work in our lives. We find these values celebrated on decorative plaques hanging on the wall in the Church lobby or Christian coffee shops. There is one virtue however, that while consistently emphasized through the entirety of the Bible, is not nearly as discussed or celebrated in modern Christian churches. I am speaking of patience, patient endurance, or long-suffering. In an age when an endless flow of self-betterment, self-empowerment, and therapeutic trends are embraced by Christian culture, very few discuss the reality that being a disciple of Jesus will be incredibly painful and difficult. Following Jesus is not a process of self-betterment; it is the process of self-denial, of "dying to self." Following Jesus well means suffering for a very, very long time. This message will never be received by the masses. As Jesus Himself said, "How narrow is the gate and difficult the road that leads to life, and few are those who find it" (Mt 7:14). The path that leads to eternal life however, is "difficult" and only a "few find it" (Mt 7:13).

When Jesus saw that "large crowds were going along with Him," He didn't cater to their desires, but instead He warned them in graphic detail that unless anyone's devotion to Him surpasses their love for their "own father and mother and wife and children and brothers and sisters, yes, and even his own life, he cannot be My disciple" (Luke 14:25-26). The reality is that the world is bursting at the seams with those who call ourselves Christians—who fully believe we are Christians, but such a small percentage of the masses have actually surrendered to a life-long marathon of dying daily. "Whoever does not carry his own cross and come after Me cannot be My disciple" (Luke 14:27). The message of the New Testament is anything but "Your Best Life Now." To the contrary, it is a life of discipline, of daily denying ourselves many of the things that we all dream of and desire now. Of course, the message of the Gospel is not perpetual denial of self, rather it is a message of delayed gratification, of "Our Best Life Then." It is a life of continually "pressing on toward the goal for the prize of the heavenly call of God in Christ Jesus" (Phil. 3:14). In the book, *Beyond the Open Door*, these values are explored in a way that not only prepares the believer for the prophesied crisis but gives biblical and dependable courage by exploring the emotions and leadership of Jesus for His church. In Matthew 24, Jesus has all out promised that there will be hatred, offenses, betrayals, deception and lawlessness, but "he who endures to the end shall be saved." How can there be salvation in the midst of such evil and what does salvation look like on that day? Jesus has promised that He will empower believers in The Evil Day, but the low hanging fruit of the oh-so-sweet Instagram-worthy self-focused platitudes of popular Christianity will end up leading many away from the hard parts of following Jesus. Not only the sugary sayings but consider the message of those who claim that the prophecies of Daniel, the book of Revelation, and many of Jesus' warnings concerning the last days were all fulfilled by AD 70. Like the false prophets of old, they assure the modern Christian that there is nothing to worry about, all these things are past; rejoice for the future is bright. Or consider the doctrine of the pre-tribulational rapture, which says that the Christian has no need to prepare their hearts to live through the great tribulation of the last days for we will all be suddenly raptured away to heaven long before any of these things come to pass. In circles where this doctrine is believed, "We're outta here anyway" has become a mantra to dismiss those who reiterate the warnings of Scripture. We could easily go on and on. These conclusions are man's attempt to wish away the scriptural admonishment to glory in tribulations, knowing that they produce perseverance; what does one need perseverance for except to endure to the end in an age when so many have been lulled to sleep by the Satanic lullabies of multiplying false prophets and teachers.

We should all be grateful for the faithful men like Gary DePasquale, true shepherds who have long been preparing the flocks of Jesus to rise to meet the great challenges that lie ahead. After reading this book, you will grow in confidence and teem with joy as you discover that the coming crisis will position the church to be unified, on fire, without spot or blemish to be victorious overcomers. I pray that the experience and the insights shared in this book will spread far and wide throughout the Body of Christ.

Maranatha.

Joel Richardson,
New York Times bestselling author, film-maker, and international teacher.

PREFACE

Beyond The Open Door is an attempt to awaken the church to a biblical reality found in scripture that has been neglected at best and redefined at worst. This biblical reality is that believers will go through the Great Tribulation, leading unto the return of Jesus, the end of the age and the age to come. This concept is not new to the scriptures nor generations of believers going back as far as the Didache manuscript[1] but foreign to many, especially within modern Christian culture due to the emergence of the prosperity gospel of the '80s and '90s and the popularity of pop theology found in Christian literature.[2] The idea of enduring the time spoken of by the ancient prophets, and even Jesus, especially within an American culture, is seen as akin to *anathema*. To consider that a generation of the church will face end-time persecution and confront the unparalleled tyranny of Satan and his Antichrist can be a terrifying concept to the escapist sensibility of the modern church. The biblical admonition to pray for strength and endure to the end is not seen in the light of all that is about to happen as time heads for the return of Jesus

---

[1] The Didache, also known as The Lord's Teaching Through the Twelve Apostles to the Nations, is a brief anonymous early Christian treatise written in Koine Greek, dated by modern scholars to the first or second century AD.

[2] Left Behind is a multimedia franchise that started with a series of sixteen bestselling religious novels by Tim LaHaye and Jerry B. Jenkins that dealt with Christian dispensationalist End Times: the pretribulation, premillennial, Christian eschatological interpretation of the Biblical apocalypse.

and the end of the age. Instead, it is seen as a way out of our everyday problems and situations.[3]

I was raised in a Bible-believing family with four generations of pastors, and I did most of my maturing in the church through the rise of televangelism, the matrimony between religion and politics, and the wide-spread airing of religious scandal and greed, and was explained as being either the attack of the devil or the blessing of the Lord. The Word of God and the Word of American Success were synonymous. A "man of God" was defined as one that possessed riches, honor, glory, and long life. There was no room for trouble, persecution, or problems in church theology—unless it was labeled as a spiritual attack or lack of faith. Both were to be overcome by praying for it to pass, reading and confessing a lot of Bible verses, or just silently ignoring it.

It was in the midst of all of the "noise" that I began to study the scriptures concerning the extraordinary time of the end of the age and the signs indicating the timing of this fast-approaching event. Now, more than ever, the church needs not to embrace ignorance but trust in God who will place us in the middle of this time of trouble as being not

---

[3] Luke 21:34-36 (New King James Version; all subsequent citations are from this version unless otherwise noted.) "But take heed to yourselves, lest your hearts be weighed down with carousing, drunkenness, and cares of this life, and that Day come on you unexpectedly. For it will come as a snare on all those who dwell on the face of the whole earth. Watch therefore, and pray always that you may be counted worthy to escape all these things that will come to pass, and to stand before the Son of Man."

only in His will but qualified as His bond servants.[4] Ignorance responds in spurn. *What good can come out of difficulty? Why would God want us to go through trouble? Jesus took the pain, so I don't have to!* Jesus said that He is returning for a glorious church without spot or wrinkle. A glorious church does not quantify God bringing good through the bad as equal to success and likability in this world. A glorious church trusts the prophetic witness in the scriptures that the church will endure persecution to make us ready to be that which Jesus is returning for: a pure and spotless bride.[5]

Jesus has promised that He will be with us always, even to the end of the age.[6] The church will not be left to flounder through the prophesied crisis of the troubled waters of persecution. We will be a victorious church that overcomes the world.[7] It will not be victory measured in treasure, but victory measured in love for Jesus. The end-time church will be triumphant in prayer and evangelism motivated by simple, unmovable devotion. We must accept the prophetic witness of the biblical prophets concerning the order of events that will bring the church to its future position and not desecrate the intended impact of perseverance on the final generation. Jesus cried over Jerusalem

---

[4] John 15:20 "Remember the word that I said to you, 'A servant is not greater than his master.' If they persecuted Me, they will also persecute you. If they kept My word, they will keep yours also."
[5] Eph. 5:27 ". . . that He might present her to Himself a glorious church, not having spot or wrinkle or any such thing, but that she should be holy and without blemish."
[6] Matt. 28:20 "'. . . teaching them to observe all things that I have commanded you; and lo, I am with you always, *even* to the end of the age.' Amen."
[7] 1 John 5:4 "For whatever is born of God overcomes the world. And this is the victory that has overcome the world—our faith."

when the religious leaders of the day rejected His Messianic claim because of the willful ignorance of the prophetic witness that did not align with their self-serving religious culture. After a series of rebukes and correctional statements found in Mathew 23:37-38 (Berean Study Bible), it ends with this final lamentation:

> O Jerusalem, Jerusalem, who kills the prophets and stones those sent to her, how often I have longed to gather your children together, as a hen gathers her chicks under her wings, but you were unwilling! Look, your house is left to you desolate.

Ignorance of the message of the biblical prophets is akin to stoning the message of the biblical prophets, and with the prophetic witness murdered, the church is left with a desolate house. Hoping everything works out is not the means to the end of the age. Being faithful to the Lord by knowing His ways and preparing accordingly is the means and the end. It is my desire to give direction and confidence through this book that will challenge our mindset to focus on what is needed and make the necessary preparations for the coming birth pangs and ultimate deliverance for all of creation.

INTRODUCTION

A Note From the Author

At the time of the writing of this book, 2020 and 2021 have been a time of unprecedented events. Parallels can be made to the 1912 political drama of Wilson versus Roosevelt, or the days of the 1918 influenza pandemic. What they did not have back then was social media. The ability to disseminate opinions and cause divisions in our day is like no time before us. This culture of division has been detrimental to the church. Great camps of disagreement surfaced through the political guise (the Trump prophecies) and the health guise (mark of the beast vaccination), not to mention the ongoing racial division that continues to plague our nation. As a pastor of a small fellowship, and the director of a night and day prayer ministry, these years were two of the most difficult of my entire time in full-time ministry. As I navigated through these cataclysms, the impact of these events upon the end-time church became evident. Through contemplation and study, it was an unusual experience that set the writing of this book into motion.

It was a Saturday morning in April of 2021 when I was preparing for a teaching the next day, not unlike any other Saturday. I usually wake up early before anyone else in the house, before even the sun breaks light. This day I woke up to an unusual darkness, it was still night. 2:38 a.m.—too early to begin my day, so I rolled over to continue my sleep. It was then that a familiar phrase rolled around in my thoughts: "Behold I have set before you an open door." Maybe it was a song. I knew it was scripture. In my attempt to sleep I found myself trying to sing a tune to this phrase, trying to find where this continuous, sleep-depriving thought was coming from, yet to no avail. I perused the different passages of scripture in my mind as this phrase kept racing against my need for sleep. I turned over once again, restless, after what seemed for minutes and looked at the clock: 2:38 a.m. I thought it was strange that time seemed to stand still. Sleep did eventually come, the time on the clock did change, and in the morning, I searched out this sleep-stealing scripture. I first turned to Revelation 4:1 that I knew spoke about a door open in heaven, but it did not seem to be the one that haunted my slumber. I then performed an internet search on the phrase, and the first suggestion to come up was Revelation 3:8. The number combination 3-8 intrigued me as it reminded me of the time on the clock that seemed to have stood still, 2:38. So, I looked it up in my

Bible: "Behold I have set before you an open door and no one can shut it."

Emotions of the early morning experience connected me to this verse. I then prayed and studied the letter written to this little church in Philadelphia, known as the Faithful Church, and thought it interesting that this statement of the open door was a recapitulation of Isaiah 22. I have read this letter of Jesus many times in the past, but now it had so much more meaning seeing it in the context of Isaiah. I wondered how Jesus was conveying a message to the faithful church of Philadelphia in the context of which He would set an open door that can never be shut. The Lord was making a statement of confidence and encouragement that would uphold the end-time church in the days of the Great Tribulation. As I continued my study, I found four doors were being highlighted, each one in the framework of the end-time scripture. Isaiah 22:22 mirrors Revelation 3:8, and they have the same context: the time of trouble. The theme of the message throughout this document is the final generation of the church facing the Great Tribulation at the hands of Satan and his Antichrist; but, the Lord Jesus Himself will hold open doors of ministry and anointing for the church that no one can shut—especially not the devil nor his emissaries. The church will grow strong in love, faith, and hope awaiting the Lord's return. These doors must be acknowledged and pursued as an act of loyalty to the Word. The Bride will be made ready and have the confidence in His end-time strategy to establish His kingdom upon the earth. This is not a matter of rapture timing or pre- or post- tribulation positions. This is not about Kingdom Now theology or the Preterist Seven-Mountain theology. This is about what the entire world is feeling. There is a big change coming to world leadership, and peoples' lives are at stake. For us in the church, we agree that there is a hostile takeover of all the kingdoms of the world on the horizon, but it is not the Antichrist that is taking over. It is THE CHRIST. We must be prepared to endure the birth pangs before we will see the birthing of this new day.

I have heard this criticism of those that recognize the coming persecution: "You are waiting for the Antichrist; we are waiting for the Christ," as if to say some people are waiting to lose while others are waiting to win. Unfortunately, the statement does not hold water. One might as well say concerning childbirth: "You are waiting for the contractions; we are waiting for the baby." The problem is that the two statements are not mutually exclusive but are indicatively connected: There is no joy of birth without the pains of labor. What is the first thing we ask a married woman if she is suddenly sick in the morning? In the same way, there is no age to come without the pains of the tribulation.[8] In the gospel of John, Jesus puts the pain of His departure within this perspective: "A woman giving birth to a child has pain because her time has come; but when her baby is born she forgets the

---

[8] 2 Thess. 2:3 "Let no one deceive you by any means; for *that Day will not come* unless the falling away comes first, and the man of sin is revealed, the son of perdition."

anguish because of her joy that a child is born into the world" (John 16:21, New International Version).

When a couple knows that they are pregnant, they begin a series of medical assessments and evaluations. They align themselves with charts concerning what a healthy birth looks like. Throughout the growth process, they are constantly checking vitals, statistics, and health. They adjust and change their diet and their activities. Their lives are in an upheaval. They participate in stretching classes and breathing classes, not for after the baby is born, but all of this is to prepare for the process of birthing. It is for the contractions that the mother prepares her body. In the same way, the church must prepare herself now before the contractions begin. Just as the father of the impending birth holds open the door to the house, the door to the car, and the door to the doctor's office, because of the changes in shape and balance of the mother, so Jesus will hold open the doors for the changing church in the end days. A mother that has entered the time of delivery without any preparation at all is considered a deficient and irresponsible mother.

The signs of the times are telling us that we must prepare for the pain of the birth just as in natural childbirth. We must be confident and function in the open doors of end-time preparedness now and throughout the time of distress. We are not called to prepare ourselves by hiding all of our money under our mattress because the banking system will be corrupted; and we are not called to store as much food and guns as we can in a secret hideaway so that we can survive the

Antichrist onslaught. Our admonition from Jesus directly related to these events is that we must lift our heads, pay attention to ourselves, keep our hearts free of sin and filled with the knowledge of Him, keep watch over the times, and pray always so that we will "be counted worthy to escape all these things that will come to pass and to stand before the Son of Man" (Luke 21:28-36).

The Lord is calling the church to walk into and function within the open doors that Jesus has set before us. These doors will never be shut. Throughout the process they will be the means through which we will be ready and prepared for the birthing. Consider this, a mother is pregnant for nine months, the birth pangs begin, and then the hard labor happens, not the whole time, but instead over hours. Then, the final act of delivery happens in a matter of minutes.

So shall it be in the last days. The church must take the time we have before the birthing to be in the proper condition to reach the actual birth. It is in this context and with anticipation for His return that I have written this book. Before you go on, I invite you to read this prayer out loud and make it your own:

Heavenly Father, I come before you prayerfully and with thanksgiving. I desire to hear from You through the pages of this book written through the weakness of a man. I ask You to pour out Your Spirit of grace and supplication that will lead Your church into all truth. Holy Spirit, lead me into Your truth for the building up of Your body and the maturity of Your people in these last days. I ask You to fill me with the knowledge of Your will in all spiritual wisdom and understanding, to walk in a manner worthy of You, fully pleasing to You, bearing fruit in every good work, and increasing in the knowledge of God. In Jesus name I humbly make this request known to You. Amen.

CHAPTER ONE

The Church of Philadelphia and Isaiah's Little Apocalypse

The subject of the end times inspires thoughts of many different characters and scenarios: the mark of the beast, the Antichrist, seven-headed creatures, the rapture, destruction, the end of the world, and many others. However, when it comes to the book of Revelation (and all scripture relating to the end times), there is one resounding conclusion that echoes through the church: It cannot be understood. One is then led to ask, why was this odd book added to the Canon of scriptures? The great monk turned reformer, Martin Luther, had a shared dislike for the book of Revelation: "To my mind it (the book of the Apocalypse) bears upon it no marks of an apostolic or prophetic character . . . Everyone may form his own judgment of this book; as for myself, I feel an aversion to it, and to me this is sufficient reason for rejecting it."[9] I believe that the reason the book of Revelation has so much confusion and aversion associated with it is because people fail to see that the vision of John is filled with recapitulations of the Old Testament prophets throughout. There are over five hundred references to the Old Testament in the book of Revelation.[10] Only the last two chapters deal with new information, but even then they still reference Old Testament concepts. Jesus used the books of Daniel and Isaiah when giving information in the Olivet Discourse of Mathew 24 and within the seven letters to the churches in Revelation chapters 2 and 3. The study of the end times must not be done in a vacuum but within the prophetic and apostolic witness of the Old Testament. The prophecies concerning the last days are scattered throughout the Pentateuch (Books of Moses) as well as the Prophets and the Psalms. The vision of John expressed in the book of Revelation finds its literary and prophetic value in putting the Old Testament prophecies in an orderly manner so that the sequence and importance of the events can be determined properly. Although there is an exhaustive amount of information in the major and minor prophets, we will be dealing with one specific prophet for the sake of this study, and that is the prophet Isaiah. Jesus gives us a very large clue as to why we must look back to Isaiah in His address to the faithful church in Revelation 3:7-13.

---

[9] Patrick F. O'Hare. *The Facts About Luther*. (Illinois: TAN Books, 1916), 203.
[10] Dr. Arnold G. Fruchtenbaum, "Old Testament References in the Book of Revelation," Accessed August 2021. http://rebel13.nl/revelation.pdf

> And to the angel of the church in Philadelphia write, "These things says He who is holy, He who is true, 'He who has the key of David, He who opens and no one shuts, and shuts and no one opens': I know your works. Behold, I have set before you an open door, and no one can shut it; for you have a little strength, have kept My word, and have not denied My name. Indeed I will make those of the synagogue of Satan, who say they are Jews and are not, but lie—indeed I will make them come and worship before your feet, and to know that I have loved you. Because you have kept My command to persevere, I also will keep you from the hour of trial which shall come upon the whole world, to test those who dwell on the earth. Behold, I am coming quickly! Hold fast what you have, that no one may take your crown. He who overcomes, I will make him a pillar in the temple of My God, and he shall go out no more. I will write on him the name of My God and the name of the city of My God, the New Jerusalem, which comes down out of heaven from My God. And I will write on him My new name. "He who has an ear, let him hear what the Spirit says to the churches."

The first thing Jesus gives to the church in Philadelphia is an allusion to the prophet Isaiah: "He who has the key of David, He who opens, and no one shuts, and shuts and no one opens." This is a claim to something that the church of Philadelphia would have recognized and responded to. The casual reader has a more difficult time in the prophetic significance within the end-time prophetic framework. Most of us, upon reading the headings, would basically conclude that the Son of God simply has an impressive title. However, to the Jewish mind, having the key of David speaks directly and distinctly to a passage of scripture that falls within what commentators call "Isaiah's Little Apocalypse."

Isaiah's prophetic writings take place during the reign of Jotham (son of King Uzziah), Ahaz, Hezekiah, and finally Hezekiah's son and successor, King Manasseh, who Isaiah was martyred by.[11] Chapter 22 of Isaiah begins with a proclamation against Jerusalem, describing both the invasion of the Assyrians and the future invasion of the Babylonians more than one hundred years in the future. However, it is also a prophecy that peers deep into the end times. It is with verse 20 that I would like to begin to build a foundation to the open doors. In order to fully value verse 20, let us examine the preceding context:

> Thus says the Lord God of hosts: "Go, proceed to this steward, to Shebna, who is over the house, and say: 'What have you here, and whom have you here, that you have hewn a sepulcher here, as he who hews himself a sepulcher on high, who carves a tomb for himself in a rock? Indeed, the Lord will throw you away violently, O mighty man, and will surely seize you. He will surely turn violently and toss you like a ball into a large country;

[11] Ancient Jewish-Christian tradition suggests that Isaiah was martyred by King Manasseh, son of Hezekiah. According to the tradition, Isaiah was tied inside a sack, placed within the hollow of a tree trunk, and then sawed in two.

> there you shall die, and there your glorious chariots shall be the shame of your master's house. So I will drive you out of your office, and from your position he will pull you down. (Isaiah 22:15-19)

The first character we are introduced to in this prophecy is Shebna, the Hebrew word for *vigor* or *life*. He is a high-ranking official given authority by King Hezekiah. Unfortunately for Shebna, he despises his position and is found ignoring the warnings from the prophets of the impending invasion coming to Israel. Instead of preparing Israel for a time of trouble, he is preparing a monument unto himself for when he dies as an old man. This action is tantamount to pride and self-absorption. No regard is given to the clear prophetic statement of the impending hardship that is coming to Israel. God deals decisively with Shebna by driving him out from the palace. He is pulled down from his position and demoted within the kingdom.

> 'Then it shall be in that day, that I will call My servant Eliakim the son of Hilkiah; I will clothe him with your robe and strengthen him with your belt; I will commit your responsibility into his hand. He shall be a father to the inhabitants of Jerusalem and to the house of Judah. The key of the house of David I will lay on his shoulder; so he shall open, and no one shall shut; and he shall shut, and no one shall open. I will fasten him as a peg in a secure place, and he will become a glorious throne to his father's house. 'They will hang on him all the glory

of his father's house, the offspring and the posterity…' (Isaiah 22:20-24)

With Shebna demoted to a place of servitude, King Hezekiah names Eliakim to not only replace Shebna but is given even greater responsibilities. Eliakim brings about the proper attitude and authority to the office, and thus he is given the highest name in the kingdom. This is signified by the laying upon his shoulder the key of the house of David. With this designation, Eliakim will carry the power and authority of the government over Israel. It involves the royal succession of David as the great doorkeeper granting or denying access to the power within the throne room. Only he can open the door of unmovable authority that no one can overrule. Eliakim in Hebrew means *God sets up*.[12] The Messianic connection is very apparent not only in the name Eliakim but in the metaphor of him being like a secure peg. The Hebrew word *aman* is translated as *secure* and is used to describe something that is well-supported, stable, assured, certain, and trustworthy—a thing in which a person can put his faith. Upon Messiah will hang all the glory of the Father. He will be steadfast and unwavering, and the glory of the Father will be shared with the offspring of Israel—the church.[13]

Shebna represents the first Adam who was the beneficiary of life by God and was given the authority of governance and dominion

---

[12] Ps. 2:6 "Yet I have set My King On My holy hill of Zion."
[13] John 17:22 (NIV) "I have given them the glory that you gave me, that they may be one as we are one . . ."

over all of creation. However, due to self-exaltation, Shebna gave up his authority and was removed from his position just as Adam shirked his responsibility and was cast down from his position in the garden. Eliakim was then set up to not only replace Shebna but to excel in his authority. In the same manner, Jesus was not only the replacement of Adam but exceeded the position and authority of Adam as described in 1 Corinthians 15:45-47:

> And so it is written, "The first man Adam became a living being." The last Adam became a life-giving spirit. However, the spiritual is not first, but the natural, and afterward the spiritual. The first man was of the earth, made of dust; the second Man is the Lord from heaven.

Jesus makes a direct connection with this event when He dictates His letter to the church of Philadelphia. The church leaders—who were more than likely Jewish—would have made this link to Isaiah and would have understood the context Jesus was drawing from. The key of David would be taken from the first and given to the last, and upon this last man would be laid the governmental authority over all of creation.[14]

As we lay this first foundation for the connection of the passage to the Messiah, we then, with confidence, continue this prophetic flow into the rest of the prophecy of Isaiah as it pertains to the letter to the

---

[14] Isa. 9:6 "For unto us a Child is born, unto us a Son is given; and the government will be upon His shoulder."

church of Philadelphia. It is in the next part of the Isaiah prophecy that we see a description of catastrophic events that will transpire during the Great Tribulation of the routing of Israel by Babylon. This in turn is an allusion to the Great Tribulation leading to the end of the age. The words of Jesus combined with the prophecy of Isaiah will give the end-time church significant direction in what is needed to endure this time, the results of this endurance, and the encouragement associated with it.

> Because you have kept My command to persevere, I also will keep you from the hour of trial which shall come upon the whole world, to test those who dwell on the earth. Behold, I am coming quickly! Hold fast what you have, that no one may take your crown. He who overcomes, I will make him a pillar in the temple of My God, and he shall go out no more. And I will write on him the name of My God and the name of the city of My God. (Revelation 3:10-12)

To properly frame the instructions of Jesus, we must understand that the acts of the Old Testament were written not only for an historical record of the dealings of Israel by God but for instruction to the church. The Bible tells us that the history of Old Testament Israel was written down and repeated for our instruction,[15] specifically the generation to whom the end of the age will come—the last days. The church has been

---

[15] Rom. 15:4 "For whatever things were written before were written for our learning, that we through the patience and comfort of the Scriptures might have hope."

a *last days entity* since Pentecost; but as we approach the close of the age, these instructions and prophetic revelations will increase as history aligns with prophecy. Although the history of Israel is for the instruction of the church, it is not unto the replacement of Israel but unto the inclusion of the church.[16] Congregations will read the Psalms liturgically and teach the little children the Old Testament "Bible stories" such as Jonah and the Whale and David and Goliath; we will decorate our newborn nurseries with Noah's Ark wallpaper, not even realizing that these are very important examples needed for instruction for the church of the end of the age. These stories cannot be relegated to the category of nursery rhymes, fables, and wall art. We must pay special attention and understand the heart of the leadership of God as we face the future crisis.

> Now all these things happened to them as examples, and they were written for our admonition, upon whom the ends of the ages have come. (1 Corinthians 10:11)

The history in the Old Testament is not only an important compilation of records but is an invaluable chronicle of experiences to be used as instructional representations applied to the prophetic operation of the plan of God's final deliverance and redemption. God has used representations and patterns in the scriptures all throughout Israel's history so that they would recognize the time of the Messiah's

---

[16] Eph. 2:11-13 ". . . being aliens from the commonwealth of Israel . . . now in Christ Jesus you who once were far off have been brought near by the blood of Christ."

coming and the transition to the age to come. It is important to take a moment to discuss the idea of biblical representations that we call metaphors.

CHAPTER TWO

End-Time Biblical Metaphors

Metaphors are an important instructional method through which the teacher will use known objects and understandings to give meaning to that which is unknown or difficult to describe. For example, when someone's personality is described as rough, it is using the word most often associated with how abrasive an object feels rather than how something is perceived. We can see this association through a display of the following two graphics: the two circles with alternating lines represent two thoughts. When brought together, the two thoughts maintain their distinction, but at the overlap, we see the alternating lines combine to make a waffle design. Within that waffle pattern the metaphor exists. It is the idea of bringing two descriptions together to produce one thought.

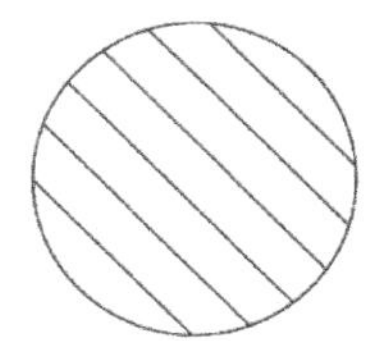
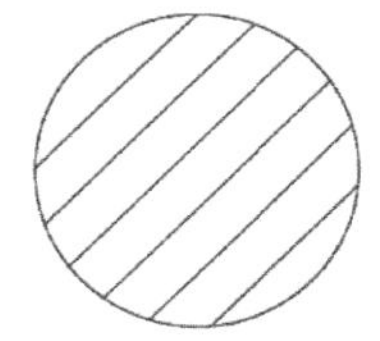
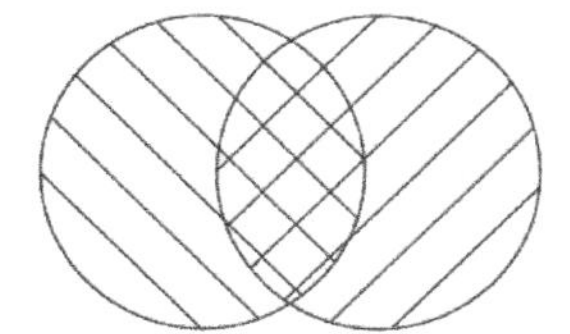

Kevin Vanhoozer's book, *Is There Meaning in this Text?,* describes the importance of hermeneutical metaphors of the scriptures as such:

> Thanks to metaphors we can set the unfamiliar in the context of the familiar in order to understand it in new ways. Metaphors may be as powerful an instrument in exploring prophetic scripture as the microscope is to science . . . by re-working language metaphors enable us to see things differently by not simply re-packaging meaning but creating it.

Metaphors have limits in that they are not meant to be an exact description of the subject. When dealing with metaphors, the reader must seek to discover what is the main idea that the metaphor is communicating rather than the truth of the example. Scripture is filled with metaphors, especially when it comes to the teachings, descriptions, and instructions to the church about the end times. I would like to explore three metaphors most used by the writers of the scripture concerning salvation and the end of the age.

All throughout the Old and New Testament, the idea of marriage between a man and a woman is used as a mystery of God's relationship with His people: Israel and the church. It is why God states that He hates divorce and made marriage exclusive for opposing sexes and not polygamous.[17] Within every marriage covenant is the metaphoric parable of the divine reality of the union between His Son and His people.[18] Every pronouncement of a human marriage performed in a devotional covenant with God is an earthly mortal image of a divine immortal plan. Human marriage within the unmovable parameters of the scripture provides language to explain not only the relationship between Christ and His people, but the emotion that drives the relationship. Pastor and author Mike Rizzo from IHOP-KC is correct in his assessment of godly marriage when he says, "Any godly character that marriage might display is essentially drawn from this heavenly partnership of God with His people, from the Garden to the Apocalypse the pattern is clear."[19]

God ultimately created marriage to be a metaphor to show the prophetic display of the end of the age. That is, the church will make herself ready as a prepared bride for her wedding day of her loving bridegroom. This is precisely why sin has so disrupted the metaphor as to make it completely indecipherable and enigmatic. The intended meaning of marriage as a consistent biblical metaphor has become an

---

[17] Gen. 2:24 "A man shall leave father and mother and be joined to his wife and the two shall become one."
[18] Eph. 5:32 "This is a great mystery, but I speak concerning Christ and the church."
[19] Longing for Eden: Embracing God's Vision in Your Marriage, 21.

affront to the godless and atheistic society of man that has embraced its fallen desire to bring disruption to any purpose of God. Man has taken marriage out from the realm of the scriptures and has hijacked it as a product of the state which then would allow a human court to define it. Marriage, as defined by the world, is no longer a message of the coming age, but as a hodgepodge of human sin and brokenness. It is of the utmost importance that believers do not give in to this modern era takeover of marriage. It was never intended to be relegated to the civil government or godless ceremonies. Marriage must always find its origin in the prophetic intention of God for the culmination of the ages.

Equal to the mystery of marriage is the mystery of labor and childbirth. This metaphor is used explicitly throughout scripture to convey sorrow and pain leading to a joyous event. Within the context of Jesus speaking to Nicodemus, the birth metaphor is used to describe a person entering into eternal life by becoming a new creation of God born from above.[20] Paul also used the metaphor of birth when referring to salvation in Christ to the Corinthian Church.[21] However, in describing the age to come, the metaphor always includes labor then birthing. One cannot have a birthing without contractions. The tell-tale sign of every birth is the contractions and the changing of the woman's body preparing her for the birthing. Hosea, Micah, Isaiah, and Jeremiah all used this striking and undeniable metaphor to describe the intensity of trouble as the birthing draws near. In every instance the prophets

[20] John 3:3 "Except a man be born again, he cannot see the kingdom of God."
[21] 2 Cor. 5:17 "Therefore if anyone is in Christ, he is a new creation."

spoke of the labor of a woman preceding a new beginning. Both Jesus and Paul used the metaphor to give purpose to the trouble that will come upon the earth heralding the return of Jesus and the Millennial Kingdom.

> But all these things are merely the beginning of birth pangs. (Matthew 24:8 New American Standard Bible 1995)

> The whole creation groans and suffers the pains of childbirth together until now. (Romans 8:22 NASB1995)

> For nation will rise up against nation, and kingdom against kingdom; there will be earthquakes in various places; there will also be famines. These things are merely the beginning of birth pangs. (Mark 13:8 NASB1995)

> While they are saying, "Peace and safety!" then destruction will come upon them suddenly like labor pains upon a woman with child, and they will not escape. (1 Thessalonians 5:3 NASB1995)

This powerful metaphor puts the church in the place of the woman in regard to what the church must endure before receiving the joy of salvation. Throughout the New Testament, we see endurance and perseverance as the main characteristics the church must pursue. Not unto a better ministry position, or a bigger church, or greater success in life, but unto greater opportunity for the gospel to go forward and shine in darkness as a light on a hill. The metaphor is used to describe endurance and perseverance through the time of the labor pains that will come upon the whole world at the end of the age.[22] The need for strength within a believer is in light of the coming trouble not in light of the coming rapture. Strength is not a prerequisite to be resurrected from the grave and to be changed in a twinkling of an eye. Strength and all its expressions are what the church should pray for in anticipation of the trial to come.

> Blessed is the man who remains steadfast under trial, for when he has stood the test he will receive the crown of life, which God has promised to those who love him. (James 1:12 English Standard Version)
>
> If we endure, we will also reign with him. (2 Timothy 2:12)
>
> But the one who endures to the end will be saved. (Matthew 24:13 ESV)

Jesus said to remember the words that He spoke, "'No servant is greater than his master.' If they persecuted Me, they will persecute you as well" (John 15:20 BSB). There must be an expectation of suffering that will come upon the church to align her with the Master. The old adage, "Jesus took the pain on the cross so I don't have to," is not only

---

[22] Heb. 10:35-39 "Therefore do not cast away your confidence, which has great reward. For you have need of endurance, so that after you have done the will of God, you may receive the promise: 'For yet a little while, *and* He who is coming will come and will not tarry. Now the just shall live by faith; but if *anyone* draws back, My soul has no pleasure in him.' But we are not of those who draw back to perdition, but of those who believe to the saving of the soul."

absent in the Bible but contrary to its unified message. The writer of Hebrews tells us that we are to fix our eyes on Jesus, the author and finisher of our faith. In the very next sentence, he tells us why: "…who for the joy that was set before him endured the cross, despising the shame" (Hebrews 12:2).

The pain before the birthing is inevitable and can only be endured with the birthing in mind. It is important for there to be an understanding of the process to bring value to the end result. It is only a recent social construct that a father joins the mother in the birthing room. In the past, he waited either in the waiting room or went home until the birth was completed. The father never knew of the pain and suffering the mother endured. The appreciation of the birthing process was lost on one-half of the relationship. Those days are long gone. Now the couple are both involved. The father to a much lesser degree, but his emotional endurance is needed in the process, even if only as a spectator of the event. Those who are expecting a child are not wanting the labor, but they know they must wait for the labor to begin before there can be a birth. Although no woman enjoys the labor after nine months of enduring body changes, health changes, and diet changes, the anticipation is palpable and contagious. Jesus once again makes this connection in regard to His soon departure from his disciples.

> Now Jesus knew that they desired to ask Him, and He said to them, "Are you inquiring among yourselves about what I said, 'A little while, and you will not see Me; and again a little while,

> and you will see Me'? Most assuredly, I say to you that you will weep and lament, but the world will rejoice; and you will be sorrowful, but your sorrow will be turned into joy. A woman, when she is in labor, has sorrow because her hour has come; but as soon as she has given birth to the child, she no longer remembers the anguish, for joy that a human being has been born into the world. Therefore you now have sorrow; but I will see you again and your heart will rejoice, and your joy no one will take from you. (John 16:19-22)

In the Olivet Discourse, Jesus uses the birthing analogy to its fullest degree in describing the time before the deliverance. He describes the events on the earth as the beginning of sorrows, or the birth pangs. As most women know best, birth pangs are the repetitive pain of a woman near the end of her pregnancy. It begins as a small twinge that increases to full-on labor as the birth process becomes inevitable. It ends with a series of pushes that release the baby into the world through the birth canal. This process is only interrupted if the mother or the child is in distress that would result in harm to either one. When this happens, then an obstetrician is required to remove the baby from the womb immediately, suddenly bringing relief to the mother and deliverance to the baby. We call that a Cesarean Section or a C-Section. This is the exact description used following the birth pangs. Jesus states in Matthew 24:22 that if the labor continues to the end, then no flesh—neither the mother nor the child—will survive, but the labor will be cut short. The Father, in a sense, will perform a Cesarean Section for the church on the Day of the Lord. At the height of the strong labor He will bring about the deliverance of the mother and the baby quickly and suddenly, ending the pain of the labor. This is what we would call the rapture of the church. First the birth pangs, then the hard labor, then the sudden deliverance. It is the use of these two metaphors combined with the teaching of Jesus, Paul, and the Apostles, that the church will face the rage of Satan during the Great Tribulation. We will be delivered out from it as Jesus, the great cloud rider, ends it with His dramatic rescue in the air. The wrath of the Lamb will follow these things.

> Hide us from the face of Him who sits on the throne and from the wrath of the Lamb! For the great day of His wrath has come and who is able to stand? (Revelation 6:16-17)

> Immediately after the tribulation of those days the sun will be darkened, and the moon will not give its light; the stars will fall from heaven, and the powers of the heavens will be shaken. Then the sign of the Son of Man will appear in heaven, and then all the tribes of the earth will mourn, and they will see the Son of Man coming on the clouds of heaven with power and great glory. And He will send His angels with a great sound of a trumpet, and they will gather together His elect from the four winds, from one end of heaven to the other. (Matthew 24:29-31)

The scriptural metaphor of *doors* is first used by God Himself and is the first use of a metaphor in human history. God said to Cain in

Genesis 4:7, “And if you do not do well, sin is crouching at the door.” The word picture is so effective in expressing the intensity of the moment within the decision that Cain is about to make. The door is closed, and if it remains closed, then sin will be kept at bay. The concept of a door keeping things in and keeping things out has been with us from the very beginning. In contrast, one of the best and most endearing biblical passages concerning open doors is found in John 10:1-10:

> "Most assuredly, I say to you, he who does not enter the sheepfold by the door, but climbs up some other way, the same is a thief and a robber. But he who enters by the door is the shepherd of the sheep. To him the doorkeeper opens, and the sheep hear his voice; and he calls his own sheep by name and leads them out. And when he brings out his own sheep, he goes before them; and the sheep follow him, for they know his voice. Yet they will by no means follow a stranger, but will flee from him, for they do not know the voice of strangers." Jesus used this illustration, but they did not understand the things which He spoke to them. Then Jesus said to them again, "Most assuredly, I say to you, I am the door of the sheep. All who ever came before Me are thieves and robbers, but the sheep did not hear them. I am the door. If anyone enters by Me, he will be saved, and will go in and out and find pasture. The thief does not come

> except to steal, and to kill, and to destroy. I have come that they may have life, and that they may have it more abundantly."

We have used the concept of doors in everyday life as idioms: If *doors are opening*, then your agenda is working; if you say *the door was closed right in my face*, then you experienced immediate and passionate rejection; if something is done *behind closed doors*, then something suspicious is operating; the metaphor is used in the sense of finality when someone is *at death's door*. One of the most dramatic uses of the metaphor is found in Psalm 24:7-10, ultimately giving description to the Messianic return of Christ.

> Lift up your heads, O you gates! And be lifted up, you everlasting doors! And the King of glory shall come in. Who is this King of glory? The Lord strong and mighty, the Lord mighty in battle. Lift up your heads, O you gates! Lift up, you everlasting doors! And the King of glory shall come in. Who is this King of glory? The Lord of hosts, He is the King of glory. Selah

Jesus uses the metaphor of the door in the last church letter, written to the Laodiceans. It is within this complete rebuke of this church that Jesus makes a plea of mercy when He says: "Behold, I stand at the door and knock. If anyone hears My voice and opens the door, I will come in to him and dine with him, and he with Me" (Revelation 3:20).

This metaphor is used to illustrate that Jesus is truly on the outside of their success when they thought He was the source of their blessings. Doors are a powerful tool of literary description, filled with meaning in the prophetic scriptures of the end of the age.

The un-shuttable door offered to the Philadelphian Church is not a promise of greater glory, greater riches, or greater honor, but a promise of opportunity. And although this verse has been used time and time again for inspirational quotes and feel-good memes, this door of promise has nothing to do with Christian bluster and bravado. It has nothing to do with a better ministry, a bigger church, or a specific calling. The end-time open doors are for the global body of Christ to assist us in overcoming the crisis ahead.

CHAPTER THREE

The Prophetic Church Letters

Teachers and pastors have spent much time and energy dissecting the letters of Paul, and rightfully so. But why is such little time given to the letters of Jesus? These letters are the direct words and thoughts of Jesus to His end-time church and contain information necessary for the church to flourish in times of trouble. There are many different personal observations made specifically to each church, but they are prophetic in nature, useful for every church in history.

In Revelation 2 and 3, Jesus constructs a series of letters addressing seven actual churches of the day. Even though they specify individual churches, the content does not pertain only to those of that era and that location. The letter addresses the church worldwide and for all periods, especially for the church that will face the end of the age events. Although each church letter is worthy of study, the sixth letter to the church of Philadelphia is our interest for the subject at hand. The congregation of Philadelphia was only one of two churches[23] that Jesus had written only affirmation and no correction. It was a strategically located trade city, colloquially known as *Little Athens,* due to its many pagan temples. It was filled with idolatry and paganistic influences whose worship dictated the success of its residents. Most of the merchants had a "pay to play" type system where the opportunities for trade were based upon the offerings given to patron gods of the different merchants. Although this affected the livelihood of so many people, Christians were at the bottom of the trading trough. Nevertheless, this church remained faithful to Jesus and the Apostles' doctrine. In a world filled with compromise, idolatry, love of money, and lovers of themselves, the church of Philadelphia stood alone and unmovable. This became their greatest achievement.

In each of His letters, Jesus gives a specific description of Himself that corresponds with their situation. To the church of Philadelphia, we find the two-fold description that He is the Holy One, meaning He is set apart as they are and that He is true, as opposed to the fictitious idols and deities of which they are surrounded by. It is the next phrase that Jesus intends to bring the reader to Isaiah 22:22: "He who has the key of David, He who opens, and no one shuts and shuts, and no one opens."

---

[23] The church of Smyrna in Revelation 2:8-11 is the other church.

This ancient hyper-link gives us the direction in which we are to understand the rest of the letter. Jesus is giving instruction to the faithful church in context to the prophecy of Isaiah in which He is implying that there is a door being opened specifically for the last days church. By keeping the scriptures and refusing to deny His name, He has qualified them to function within the door that is open in spite of the challenges that they find themselves in. If we were to look at the résumé of this church, the natural man would not put much stock in them: small membership, not redefining the scriptures for the sake of culture, intense loyalty to the reality of Jesus, and radical perseverance in persecution. These do not typically make the list of most western church growth principles. Take a moment and think about this: Jesus opens every letter with His intimate knowledge of each church. If you are a church leader, what kind of letter do you think He would write to you about the church you have been given charge over? Selah.

The letter to the Philadelphian Church, the crux of this study, is sandwiched between two other letters addressed to Sardis and Laodicea—of which Jesus had nothing good to say about; but Philadelphia had nothing but praise. Not only is the letter to Philadelphia between the letters of Sardis and Laodicea but geographically it is the same.

Philadelphia, in Asia Minor, is now a Turkish city called Alaşehir. In the days of the letter from Jesus, it was a Greek colony called the Gateway to the East. It was established to spread Greek culture into the eastern Asia minor region. The church was founded during the missionary journeys of Paul in AD 46-48 and had been functioning as such for over forty years when they received the letter from Jesus. The church stayed in existence for the next millennia until it was finally overrun by the Ottoman Empire in the fourteenth century. Today, the ruins of this church are still evident but limited to a couple of foundation stones and worn and crumbled pillars that held up the portico.

At the close of the first century this church was marked by Jesus. They had kept His Word and had done everything Jesus said to do. What joy it must have been for Jesus to say that of this little synagogue. The key to success is to have that affirmation be alive in you. In the last days, it will be of the utmost importance for the end-time church to be characterized as doing everything He says and being everything that He wants, in accordance with His Word. It is not complicated to know what those things are. We just need to look at the book of Acts once again: "And they continued steadfastly in the apostles' teachings and fellowship, in the breaking of bread [communion] and the prayers" (Acts 2:42, American Standard Version).

Jesus continued the commendations that they did not deny the honor and glory due Him, not in worship songs and hymns alone but in activity and testimony to the culture in which they lived. They kept the command of Jesus to be patient. The Greek word for patience is *hupomone,* and here is the precise definition as taken from the Greek Lexicon:

1. steadfastness, constancy, endurance, a patient, steadfast waiting
    a. in the New Testament the characteristic of a man who is not swerved from his deliberate purpose and his loyalty to faith and devotion by even the greatest trials and sufferings

Patience is an attribute of the end-time church that will be most needed. The word does not speak of patience as waiting with inactivity but patience when experiencing trials. This is what will be required of the church during the end-time persecution. In the letters, we see that it is not a suggestion but a command with a promise: "Because you have kept My command to persevere, I also will keep you from the hour of trial which shall come upon the whole world, to test those who dwell on the earth" (Revelation 3:10).

The command to persevere is not the trial but is the attribute needed that will keep us from the intended result of the trial. Since this is a command, Jesus will empower His followers with the ability to obey to its fullness.[24] The phrase "hour of trial that will come upon the whole world" is in contention among scholars as to whether it is the Great Tribulation or the Day of the Lord. It is my position that it is a reference to the time just before the return of Jesus in the midst of the

[24] John 14:15 (The Passion Translation) "Loving me [Jesus] empowers you to obey my commands."

Great Tribulation. Waiting for deliverance from any trial is very difficult to do in your own strength. Andrew Brunson spent twenty-four years as an American Missionary to Turkey and was finally freed from a Turkish prison in October 2018 after 735 days in captivity because of false accusations that came against his faith. In his book, *God's Hostage*, he gives a primary example of patience and perseverance in the intensity of a real trial:

> I realized I could not do much to fight for my freedom, but I would fight for my faith. If I do not survive spiritually, I knew I would lose everything. I had spent so many hours pacing the courtyard or lying on my bunk, accusing God, confused and often angry and offended at him. But now I made a solemn decision, and announced it to God, almost in defiance: Whatever you do or do not do, I will follow you. This became the basis of my declaration and I added to it. If you do not speak to me, I will follow you. If you do not let me sense your presence; I will follow you. If you do not show your gentleness or kindness, I will follow you. If you allow me to be deceived, I will follow you. If you leave me in prison, I will follow you! I had no illusion that I could make it without God's help. But insofar as it was up to me, I determined to persevere. I made a decision: I will not give up! I may be terrified, I may be weak, I may be broken, but I am going to hold on. I will look to Jesus,

not away from him, I will run to Jesus or, if necessary, crawl to Jesus.[25]

People tend to be impatient when we do not see the results we expect or if the results we expect become delayed. We measure success by how fast something grows, or how soon something is established. This is because we embrace existentialism rather than an eschatological-ism. It shows in our preaching and teaching and presentations of the gospel. Existentialists live for this age while eschatologists live for the age to come. The church is more popular when they are focused on delivering people from their hang-ups rather than from hell. The American Church is too preoccupied with striving to answer the personal and political problems of the present. Thus, we overlook the endeavoring of the setting of our minds on things ahead of us.[26] The church is to be an eschatological people. If understood properly, this mindset would profoundly affect how we deal with the problems of the present.

All scriptures that mention patience concern the coming of the Lord and the age to come. Patience is not about simply following a virtue; it is the training ground for trials—specifically eschatological trials. This is one of the reasons why the American church is anemic and susceptible to the same failures the world falls prey to. We are

---

[25] Andrew Brunson, *God's Hostage.* (Grand Rapids, Baker Publishing Group, 2019), 159.
[26] Col. 3:2 (BSB) "Therefore, since you have been raised with Christ, strive for the things above, where Christ is seated at the right hand of God. Set your minds on things above, not on earthly things."

living for the wrong age! I have personally garnered criticism in the pursuit of raising up night and day prayer, but the most criticism I have received comes from the consistent teaching concerning the last days scriptures. I make no apologies, nor do I counter the criticism because I believe we are in a last generation situation that requires "Ezekiel 33 Shepherds" to emphasize the closing of this present evil age. We are to be the generation to declare the birthing of the Messianic age.

> Son of man, give your people this message: 'When I bring an army against a country, the people of that land choose one of their own to be a watchman. When the watchman sees the enemy coming, he sounds the alarm to warn the people. Then if those who hear the alarm refuse to take action, it is their own fault if they die. They heard the alarm but ignored it, so the responsibility is theirs. If they had listened to the warning, they could have saved their lives. But if the watchman sees the enemy coming and doesn't sound the alarm to warn the people, he is responsible for their captivity. They will die in their sins, but I will hold the watchman responsible for their deaths.' Now, son of man, I am making you a watchman for the people of Israel. Therefore, listen to what I say and warn them for me. (Ezekiel 33:2-7 New Living Translation)

The church of Philadelphia was obeying the Word of God. They were courageous in not denying His name. They waited patiently for the things of God in the future. They outlasted every other church in antiquity.[27]

Jesus celebrates the church of Philadelphia and has no correction for them. He praises them for their tenacity, but instead of offering up a respite for them, He describes the opposition that is yet to come. Jesus infuses them with boldness and prepares them for more intense trouble that will be coming as they continue to pursue Him. He promises what they are about to face will not thwart their momentum at all, but on the contrary, Jesus Himself will hold open the door of their ministry assignments unto His return. His promise says to them that if they are operating within the open door, then no one will stop its effectiveness until the end.

---

[27] The only other church that survived the test of time is Smyrna which also had no correction from Jesus and dealt with persecution from the Synagogue of Satan.

CHAPTER FOUR

The Expectation of Overcoming

Throughout all of the different distinctions that Jesus cites in assisting each church to come into alignment, there is one phrase that is used that unifies all seven churches: "to him who overcomes." This phrase is not to be only understood as each church overcoming their current situations or overcoming their present challenges, but it is an eschatological statement made primarily to the church of the last days. Some have taught these letters to be seven dispensations of the church throughout history with the last letter showing the complete compromise of the church applied to the time of history we find ourselves in today. This kind of understanding does a great disservice to the text and to the intentions of the author, Jesus. A more plausible dissemination of the letters is that they are cumulative in nature. All seven attitudes will exist in the last days church. To simply say that only the compromised Laodicean spirit of the seventh letter is what exemplifies today's church is something that I consider out of the bounds of proper hermeneutics for apocalyptic writings. The letter must be understood within the structure of a normal, natural, customary hermeneutic that says thus: To whom was the promise made? What were the conditions when the promise was made? How can it be applied now? This is the crux of the matter.

At the writing of this book, the United States has pulled out all troops from Afghanistan. The Taliban has taken over the capital city of Kabul and deposed the sitting president. They have stopped all outgoing air travel as a means of escape, leaving the church of the region in grave danger. There are already reports of soldiers going from house to house with lists of names and locations of Afghan congregations, a church body that has been one of the fastest growing in the world. Consider this report by Yahoo news concerning the dire situation:

> ISIS killers are now joining the ranks of the Taliban, ignoring their differences until all infidels are caught, tortured, and killed. They have names of people who have converted to Christianity and are aggressively searching them out. These Christians are not afraid to die, but want their children to live and live free. The

> resources are there, courage is on a dramatic rise, and the will is strong, but chaos and evil have been waiting for this moment.[28]

Can you imagine those house church leaders gathering under threat of murder and rape watching a YouTube recording of a preacher in America describing how the church of these last days is described as having a Laodicean spirit? Can you imagine them listening to a preacher that is saying, "The church will be raptured before the trouble begins because God would not allow His Bride to be a battered wife?"[29] We must understand that the letters of Jesus are cumulative in effect and are prescriptive for the last days church to receive admonition and correction.

Two of the seven churches only received commendation, and both of them were experiencing persecution: the church of Smyrna and the church of Philadelphia.

> "And to the angel of the church in Smyrna write, 'These things says the First and the Last, who was dead, and came to life: I know your works, tribulation, and poverty (but you are rich); and I know the blasphemy of those who say they are Jews and are not, but are a synagogue of Satan. Do not fear any of those things which you are about to suffer. Indeed, the devil is about to throw some of you into prison, that you may be tested, and

---

[28] "GCM Offers New Statement from Afghanistan's Underground Church," Yahoo! Finance, August 25, 2021.
[29] This was an actual statement made by a professor of theology in a major seminary.

you will have tribulation ten days. Be faithful until death, and I will give you the crown of life. He who has an ear, let him hear what the Spirit says to the churches. He who overcomes shall not be hurt by the second death." (Revelation 2:8-11)

The letters to Smyrna and Philadelphia have in common the ongoing trouble and lack of resources in their fellowship. Smyrna was a port city and Philadelphia was about ninety miles inland. At the time, they were well within the empire of Rome until it was finally besieged by Mehmed II the Conqueror and the Ottoman Turks in 1453. In His letter, Jesus immediately acknowledged that He knew that they were facing persecution by the same group of people of whom Jesus called the synagogue of Satan. Although these verses have been used to justify hatred against all Jews or particular subsets of Jews, scholarly academia has considered this ignorant of the biblical context and the intended prophetic nature of this designation. Although there is no direct evidence of this particular title associated with the persecutors of the time of the letters, Jesus seems to be using a descriptive title expressing the attitude of those that are oppressing them. This is not secular or paganistic persecution but a religious persecution arguing against the authenticity of the church as following the God of Abraham, Isaac, and Jacob. In using a descriptive title rather than an actual named group, we are allowed to then apply this persecution to a modern day understanding.

CHAPTER FIVE

The Synagogue of Satan

I feel it is important to focus here upon this often ignored portion of the Philadelphia letter concerning the Synagogue of Satan. My intention is not to scrutinize the text to discover the "villain" but rather to identify this group because of the great awakening that will take place among them. For this reason, the letters of Jesus taken as a cumulative instruction for the last days church leads us to investigate this mysterious persecutor mentioned in the letter to Smyrna and Philadelphia. Understanding who this group might be will encourage the end-time church to be prepared with expectation to receive them during the time of the great and final harvest.

Although the Synagogue of Satan was more than likely an actual group of people that were persecuting the church at that time, it was not a name of a certain place or certain gathering, such as the First Church of the Resurrection. However, since the passage is prophetic in nature, it is also informative in its description so that it can be recognized throughout the annals of time leading up to the last days. In the first century, when the letters of Jesus were given, there was not a distinct designation between Christianity and Judaism. Instead, the ecclesia of that day was called The Way[30] and comprised Jews who accepted Jesus as their Messiah, thus becoming born again.[31] It is known from the book of Acts that Saul was part of a group commissioned to persecute the sect called The Way, and he oversaw the persecution and murder of many. However, after Saul's conversion, the persecution of The Way continued, and Saul, known as Paul, would preach to his once fellow persecutors and see them come out from among the oppressors to become born again, although many continued in their persecution.[32] After the Diaspora, following the destruction of the temple in AD 70 and the Bar Kokhba Revolt (AD 132-136), the face of Judaism changed. Rabbinic Judaism became a religion centered around synagogues due to the destruction of the temple. Jews were dispersed out of Jerusalem and to the far reaches of the Roman world and beyond.[33] Hadrian (Roman Emperor AD 117–138) attempted to

[30] The Way is mentioned six times in the book of Acts in connection with early followers of Jesus. They were one of several sects of Judaism

[31] John 3:3 Jesus, a Rabbi, speaking to Nicodemus, a Pharisee: "…unless one is born again he cannot see the kingdom of God."

[32] Acts 19:1-10

[33] Rabbi Nosson Dovid Rabinowhich (ed.), The Iggeres of Rav Sherira Gaon, Jerusalem 1988, 6.

completely root out Judaism which he saw as the cause of continuous rebellions. The Torah and the Hebrew calendar were then prohibited. Judaic scholars were executed. The sacred scroll was ceremonially burned on the Temple Mount. At the former Temple sanctuary, two statues were erected: one of Jupiter and one of Emperor Hadrian. To erase any memory of Judea and Ancient Israel, the names were wiped off the map and replaced with Syria-Palaestina. Similarly, Hadrian reestablished Jerusalem as the Roman polis of Aelia Capitolina and all Jews were barred from entering the city.[34] As the Jews scattered, the Gentiles stayed, and the Jewish sect called The Way would now see its makeup change from being predominantly Jewish to a more Gentile presence. The persecution of the Jews eliminated the traditions of Semitic origins within the church, thereby cultivating a cultural vacuum and infusing regional perspectives into new traditions for fear of expulsion by Rome. For instance, the Feast of the Dedication (Hanukkah) is celebrated on the Hebrew month of Kislev, on the twenty-fifth day. Kislev occurs about the same time as the Roman month of December. It is quite possible that the predominantly Gentile church covered up their outlawed celebration of Hanukkah by instituting December 25th as a celebration of light in the temple. Since anything Jewish was prohibited, eventually that observance changed into the celebration of the light of the world that was eventually marked

---

[34] H.H. Ben-Sasson, *A History of the Jewish People.* (Cambridge: Harvard University Press, 1976), 334.

as the birth of Christ. This is not definitively historical, but there are some ancient manuscripts that suggest this to be factual.

With the teachings of Paul to the Gentiles, and the clear ministry of Jesus to the House of Israel, we see now that today's Christianity will experience a *one new man* transformation in the last days in which the unity seen in The Way will be seen once again before the coming of Jesus. The last days church will be focused on the importance of their Jewish roots as Jews looking for the spiritual significance of their faith will embrace the idea of Jesus as the prophesied Messiah. This awakening will change the face of Christianity and Judaism back to the understanding—and the inclusion—of the unified body of Messiah. I would like to quote my good friend, Rabbi Jack Jacobs's article, entitled Messiah's Mutual Mandate, in regard to this awakening:

> In Deuteronomy 32:43 we find this direct instruction spoken by Moses to the Nations, "Rejoice, O nations, with His people". This is a simple, yet profound exhortation to the Gentiles of every Nation who believe and obediently follow the God of Abraham, Isaac and Jacob to be rejoicing with the Jewish people! In Romans chapter 15 Paul, the Apostle to the Gentiles, cites this same passage from Deuteronomy, as well as other passages from the Old Covenant that clearly confirm God's desire for the Nations to be relationally involved with the Jewish people. The Apostle Paul quotes this Hear O Nations passage in order to explain the important spiritual calling and

> destiny of the Gentile believers to bind themselves in rejoicing with Israel, God's Chosen People. By directly quoting Moses (from Deuteronomy 32:43), Isaiah (from Isaiah 11:10) and David (from Psalm 18:49 and Psalm 117:1). Paul compellingly calls for the unity God desires for every Jewish and Gentile believer in Messiah Yeshua: "Therefore, accept one another, just as Messiah also accepted us to the glory of God. For I say that Messiah has become a servant to the circumcision on behalf of the truth of God to confirm the promises given to the fathers, and for the Gentiles to glorify God for his mercy; as it is written, 'Therefore I will give praise to you among the Gentiles, and I will sing to your name.' Again, he says, 'Rejoice, O Gentiles, with his people.' and again, 'Praise the Lord all you Gentiles, and let all the peoples praise him.' Again Isaiah says, 'There shall come the root of Jesse, and he who arises to rule over the Gentiles, in him shall the Gentiles hope.' now may the God of hope fill you with all joy and peace in believing, so that you will abound in hope by the power of the Holy Spirit." (Romans 15:7-13)[35]

This article represents the sentiment of the one new man in the last days. Jews and Gentiles making large prophetic strides in this declaration of the Holy Spirit of unity. In the days of the promised

[35] 2021 article published in Tikkun America e-magazine

Great Harvest at the end of the age,[36] there will be multitudes of Jews and Gentiles coming to faith in Yeshua as Messiah and will grow in strength and number to truly embrace the Romans 11:17 admonition: "You, being a wild olive tree, were grafted in among them, and with them became a partaker of the root and fatness of the olive tree."

This promised end-time awakening will disqualify the modern Jewish Synagogue to be the Synagogue of Satan as an end-time persecutor of the church because the church will once again have a mutual expression of both Jew and Gentile as the one new man directive implies. This is not to say that Judaism will no longer exist, nor do I mean to suggest that the church will be absent of Jewish disagreement and/or persecution, or that every Jewish person will be a part of the one new man reality; but there will be a significant number of Jewish people that will receive an understanding of Yeshua and an unprecedented turnaround will occur as Jews and Christians return to their first love of the church. With this revelation, Judaism will truly be the root system of the Christian Church, and the return back to its foundation of the apostles and prophets will occur.

> Therefore remember that you, once Gentiles in the flesh—who are called Uncircumcision by what is called the Circumcision made in the flesh by hands—that at that time you were without

---

[36] Rev. 7:9-10 ". . . behold, a great multitude which no one could number, of all nations, tribes, peoples, and tongues, standing before the throne and before the Lamb, clothed with white robes, with palm branches in their hands . . ."

> Christ, being aliens from the commonwealth of Israel and strangers from the covenants of promise, having no hope and without God in the world. But now in Christ Jesus you who once were far off have been brought near by the blood of Christ. For He Himself is our peace, who has made both one, and has broken down the middle wall of separation, having abolished in His flesh the enmity, that is, the law of commandments contained in ordinances, so as to create in Himself one new man from the two, thus making peace, and that He might reconcile them both to God in one body through the cross, thereby putting to death the enmity. And He came and preached peace to you who were afar off and to those who were near. For through Him we both have access by one Spirit to the Father. Now, therefore, you are no longer strangers and foreigners, but fellow citizens with the saints and members of the household of God, having been built on the foundation of the apostles and prophets, Jesus Christ Himself being the chief cornerstone, in whom the whole building, being joined together, grows into a holy temple in the Lord, in whom you also are being built together for a dwelling place of God in the Spirit. (Ephesians 2:11-22)

Who then holds the credentials to be the last days persecutor of both Jew and Gentile? "I will cause some belonging to Satan's synagogue who say that they themselves are Jews, and are not, but are liars" (Revelation 3:9).

Replacement theology is summed up in the term super-secessionism: the idea that God has rejected Israel as His chosen people and has replaced them with another entity. Throughout church history large parts of Christianity held to this idea of super-secessionism, although it has waned since the establishment of national Israel in 1948. However, one major religion with millions of followers still holds to that ideology very strongly: that religion is Islam.

Unlike traditional super-secessionism, Islam does not hold to a *replacement theory* but a *displacement theory.* They do not see themselves as being the "New Israel;" instead, it recasts the Jewish prophets as Muslim by creating a direct link with Ishmael, a son of Abraham through Haggar[37] as the "first Muslim," according to the Quran. Muhammad originally desired to bring the Jews within the fold of Islam. He accepted the Jewish God and prophets and many Jewish practices, initially including the orientation of prayers toward Jerusalem. The affinity for the Jews as the "Chosen People" and for the land as their "Promised Land" is acknowledged in the Quran.[38]

When Muhammad first began visiting Mecca there were numerous Jews living there through years of migration due to the multiple conquests of Jerusalem. These Jewish communitites played a significant role during the rise of Islam and at first enjoyed the

---

[37] Gen. 16
[38] Quran, 2:47 and 122, 17:104, 10:93

interfaith sentiment of Mohammed and his followers. Later, Muhammad encountered opposition from the Jews as he began to prop himself up as a sage and a prophet to instruct them in new revelations. As his proselytizing became more aggressive, the Jews rejected him altogether and considered him a heretic. This began the growing negative view of Jews and Christians within the Islamic faith. Many of Muhammad's first ayas (verses) were positively addressed to Jews in an attempt to win them to adopt the Quran in addition to the Torah. After realizing that the Jews were not going to join his new version of Judaism, Muhammad proceeded to establish a separate religion. From that point on, the relations with his Jewish neighbors deteriorated quickly. Mecca, not Jerusalem, was made the holy city, and Muhammad's converts were required to pray towards this Jerusalem replacement. In AD 628, Muhammad attacked the Jewish communitites, dispossessing, enslaving, exiling, and massacring them.[39] It is in Sura 5 of the Quran, written after the massacre, where we would find the Muslim doctrine of supersession. The commentator's explain that Islam remedies "the backsliding of the Jews and Christians from their pure religions to which the coping stone was placed by Islam."[40] This is known in the traditional Islamic commentary as "the memorable declaration" (Surah 5:3): "This day have I perfected your religion for you, completed my favor upon you, and have chosen for you Islam as

---

[39] Paul Johnson, *History of the Jews.* (New York: Harper & Row, 1987), 167.
[40] Abdullah Yusuf Ali, "The Absolute Reality,"
http://www.quran4u.com/Tafsiraya/005%20Ma'ida.pdf

your religion."[41] The verse puts it bluntly: the favor of Allah, which went initially to the Jews, has moved in its perfected form to Islam.

In making this proposition that the identity of the persecutors is Islam, I would like to stress that I am not an expert in the doctrines of Islam as to be considered an authority. However, I have gathered my information and insight through known scholars and authors some of whom I have sat at a table with for discussion and who are very well versed on the subject of Islam.[42] To my knowledge, I have not heard of any making this connection of Islam and the Synagogue of Satan, and I understnd that this suggestion is one that would garnish much criticism. It is therefore my intention to present my assumptions in this chapter as one that is confident yet humble in its conclusion. Although this could be viewed as a strong charge concerning Islam, it is not without precedent regarding their approaches toward Judaism and Christianity. Many popular and well-known Imams have expressed oppression against Jews and Chrsitians openly as have many leaders of Islamic Nations. However, this in no way should constitute an attack on Muslim individuals. Not all Muslims consider persecution as a means of their belief system, and many Muslims are very delightful and peace-loving people. We should not take this as permission to categorize anyone into a particular ideology, but we must, as believers, be hospitable and personal with everyone with the hopes that we may win some to the

---

[41] Introduction to sura 5 in the popular Saudi edition The Qur'an: King Fahd's Holy Qur'an (Saudi Arabia: The Royal Palace, 2000).
[42] For more information on the part Islam may play in the end time scriptures, I would encourage you to purchase *Antichrist: Islam's Awaited Messiah* by Joel Richardson.

Lord. I believe that an unprecedented amount of Muslims will come to the saving knowledge of Jesus as the Jewish Messiah within the great end-time harvest.

It is on this basis that I can sum up my conclusion. In Revelation 3:9, the Synagogue of Satan of the end-time church is none other than Islam itself. Their own writings make the declaration that they have replaced the Jews as God's chosen people. In a sense, they are declaring themselves as Jews through claiming Abraham as their father, although they would not consider themselves Jewish. In the letter, Jesus makes a powerful phrase about the claim of the Synagogue of Satan: "[they] say they are Jews and are not, but lie." (Revelation 3:9). The two words "but lie" are translated from *Alla Pseúdomai*, meaning, these people are declaring falsehoods.[43] They do not do so from a motivation of purposeful deception but from a sincere heart that has been purposely deceived by Satan. It is because of the justice and mercy of God, that the God of Ishmael, who is Elohim, will fulfill His promise and will respond to the voice of Ishmael once again:

> When the water was gone, she [Hagar] put the boy [Ishmael] in the shade of a bush. Then she went and sat down by herself about a hundred yards away. "I don't want to watch the boy die," she said, as she burst into tears. But God heard the boy crying, and the angel of God called to Hagar from heaven,

---

[43] Although not a direct translation meaning a deity, the author finds it interesting that the Greek word for "but" in Revelation 3:9 is the word "alla."

> "Hagar, what's wrong? Do not be afraid! God has heard the boy crying as he lies there. Go to him and comfort him, for I will make a great nation from his descendants." Then God opened Hagar's eyes, and she saw a well full of water. She quickly filled her water container and gave the boy a drink. And God was with the boy. (Genesis 21:15-20 NLT)

The God of Abraham has not left the descendants of Ishmael and is still desiring to restore to them the status of a great nation under His covering. The Arab nations will see a great revival as the Lord opens their eyes as He did with Hagar and they will see the well filled with the water of the Holy Spirit.

In that context, let us now look at this same verse using the Aramaic Bible in Plain English Version: "And behold, I grant <u>some</u> of the synagogue of Satan, of those who say about themselves that they are Jews and are not, but they are lying, behold, I shall make them <u>come and worship before your feet</u> and to know that I love you" (Revelation 3:9).

We see the use of the word *ek* translated as "some" of those belonging to Satan's Synagogue will come to the church to worship Jesus with them "before their feet." This phrase is not meant to show vindication but is to be seen as those that will worship the true God as of disciples listening to their teacher's instruction that are said to be at his feet. This accentuates the idea that some of the persecutors will see the error of their ways, come to the saving knowledge of Jesus, and join the church in their worship of the true God of Ishmael

> Behold, I will cause them, so that they will come and will worship in sight of your feet and they shall know that I have loved you. (Revelation 3:9 Literal Emphasis Translation)

This is happening throughout the Islamic world right now as many Muslims are being visited in a dream or a vision by a man they have called a "man in white."[44] They are leaving the mosques even under threat of death and joining other believers, worshiping the Lord side by side with them, learning the ways of the God of Abraham, Issac and Jacob.

> Because you have kept My command to persevere, I also will keep you from the hour of trial which shall come upon the whole world, to test those who dwell on the earth. Behold, I am coming quickly! Hold fast what you have, that no one may take your crown. (Revelation 3:10-11)

The promise then continues in the letter that through the perseverance of the church during the time of persecution, they are promised to be "kept out of" or "carefully taken care of" (Greek: *tereo*) during the time of trial that will come upon the whole earth. This passage has been used by pretribulationalists to support the view that the church will be spared from going through what they consider as a

---

[44] Darren Carlson, "When Muslims Dream of Jesus," *International Mission News*, May 31, 2018, https://www.thegospelcoalition.org/article/muslims-dream-jesus/.

seven-year tribulation period. The text does give a promise of Jesus that believers will be kept from experiencing the full weight of the hour of trial; but what does the phrase "keep out of" actually mean? This verse has been highly debated for many years, but one just needs to look at the other use of the Greek word *tereo* in John 17:15 to have a clearer understanding: "I do not pray that You should take them out of the world, but that You should keep them from the evil one."

The word "keep" is used here in the High Priestly prayer of Jesus and is the only other passage where the same construction is used as in Revelation 3:10. It is clear that the keeping is not out from the world but to be carefully taken care of in the midst of the activities of the evil one. Since John wrote both of the passages under consideration, and both are quotes from Jesus Himself, it makes sense to interpret them similarly. The promise of Jesus is to take care of and strengthen believers from within the trial. This is why our trust level in the face of afflictions must be exercised regularly. This hour of testing is still yet to come and is not limited to Jerusalem or Israel but will come upon the "whole world."[45] Paul wrote about the importance of our trials that we experience now as precursors to that which is to come. I would like to close this chapter with a very significant passage of scripture that has ministered to me time and time again.

---

[45] For further investigation I recommend the book *Revelation Bombshell* by Charles Cooper, Strong Tower Publishing, 2012.

But we have this treasure in earthen vessels, that the excellence of the power may be of God and not of us. We are hard-pressed on every side, yet not crushed; we are perplexed, but not in despair; persecuted, but not forsaken; struck down, but not destroyed—always carrying about in the body the dying of the Lord Jesus, that the life of Jesus also may be manifested in our body. For we who live are always delivered to death for Jesus' sake, that the life of Jesus also may be manifested in our mortal flesh. So then death is working in us, but life in you. And since we have the same spirit of faith, according to what is written, "I believed and therefore I spoke," we also believe and therefore speak, knowing that He who raised up the Lord Jesus will also raise us up with Jesus, and will present us with you. For all things are for your sakes, that grace, having spread through the many, may cause thanksgiving to abound to the glory of God. Therefore, we do not lose heart. Even though our outward man is perishing, yet the inward man is being renewed day by day. For our light affliction, which is but for a moment, is working for us a far more exceeding and eternal weight of glory, while we do not look at the things which are seen, but at the things which are not seen. For the things which are seen are temporary, but the things which are not seen are eternal. (2 Corinthians 4:7-18)

There is a great revival coming to every nation, but it will not come without many tribulations. The second century apologist Quintus Tertullian wrote "the blood of the martyrs is the seed of the church," and we will see the end-time persecutors of the people of God become the end-time lovers of God. I would ask you to find ways to remember our brothers and sisters all over the world who are facing martyrdom today because of their faith and pray for many to come into the kingdom through their sacrifice.

CHAPTER SIX

The Open Door of Night and Day Prayer

As was stated back in Chapter 1 of this book, Jesus has promised that He will keep an open door for the end-time church to endure and persevere through a time of persecution known as the Great Tribulation. In the beginning of the letter, we see Jesus referencing Isaiah 22:22 as the context by which He will act in accordance with the faithful church. The door that He mentions is not a generic door, nor is it a door of opportunity for the believer to gain glory, riches, honor and long life. It is a specific door by which those who enter it—regardless of their strength or impact—will be assisted in the endurance required during the hour of trial. There is prophetic scripture concerning the functions of the end-time church we ought to be perusing now before that evil day.[46]

Because Jesus references Isaiah 22 as the basis in which He desires to interact with the end-time church, we have considered it an invitation to go back to the prophecy of Isaiah associated with His descriptive titles and search out Jesus' leadership. Isaiah's prophecy will give us insight into the functions of the church that will aid her with endurance despite the challenging conditions described.

We will pick up the unfolding drama with the passage in Isaiah 24 where the descriptions and suggestions seem to reference a time of great tribulation. Isaiah begins this chapter by filling thirteen verses of expressive desolation upon the land and the people. Descriptions pepper the text such as, "the land shall be plundered; the earth is defiled under its inhabitants; the cities are in desolation." He says it looks like the shaking of an olive tree. Then the narrative takes an unexpected turn. We see that there is a remnant of people who respond amid the chaos. The first response of this faithful throng is found in Isaiah 24:14-16:

> They shall lift up their voice, they shall sing; for the majesty of the Lord they shall cry aloud from the sea. Therefore, glorify the Lord in the dawning light, the name of the Lord God of Israel in

---

[46] Eph. 6:13 "Therefore take up the whole armor of God, that you may be able to withstand in the evil day, and having done all, to stand."

> the coastlands of the sea. From the ends of the earth we have heard songs: "Glory to the righteous One!"

It is here that we see the first door that will be un-shuttable on that day and will remain open hastening His return.

The concept of night and day prayer is not just a ministry fad that attracts musicians, singers, and songwriters. Jesus was extremely passionate and discriminate concerning the centralized place of continuous intercessory worship. We see Him twice in His ministry on the earth cleansing the temple and reestablishing it as the centralized place of prayer and worship.

During the time of the Great Tribulation, the most emphasized cry of believers and unbelievers alike will be *justice*. From unbelievers, it will be a cry to the courts, to the government, and to the media, but they will not find any relief. Believers will summon a higher court and the righteous Judge will respond. The Lord has set up a system that will be catalytic across the earth in releasing God's justice onto principalities and powers that influence the kings of the earth to help propagate the trouble. In the tenth chapter of Isaiah, it speaks of the Assyrian who shall strike with a rod and lift his staff in violence.[47] The admonition of the Lord is to not be afraid when this happens. Within that context he gives the description of the counter offensive by the faithful church:

---

[47] Isa. 10:5 "Woe to Assyria, the rod of My anger and the staff in whose hand is My indignation."

> And in that day, you will say: "Praise the Lord, call upon His name; declare His deeds among the peoples, make mention that His name is exalted. Sing to the Lord, for He has done excellent things; this is known in all the earth. Cry out and shout, O inhabitant of Zion, for great is the Holy One of Israel in your midst!" (Isa. 12:1-6)

The consistent calling upon the people of God during the time of trouble is to sing, worship, and declare the wonders of the Lord. Again, we see this interaction repeated in the story of King Jehoshaphat in 2 Chronicles 20. The armies of Moab and Ammon came to battle against Israel. Jehoshaphat was fearful and called a fast throughout all of Judah.

> After this, the Moabites and Ammonites with some of the Meunites came to wage war against Jehoshaphat. Some people came and told Jehoshaphat, “A vast army is coming against you from Edom, from the other side of the Dead Sea. It is already in Hazezon Tamar” (that is, En Gedi). Alarmed, Jehoshaphat resolved to inquire of the LORD, and he proclaimed a fast for all Judah. The people of Judah came together to seek help from the LORD; indeed, they came from every town in Judah to seek him. Then Jehoshaphat stood up in the assembly of Judah and Jerusalem at the temple of the LORD in the front of the new courtyard and said: “LORD, the God of our ancestors, are you not the God who is in heaven? You rule over all the kingdoms

of the nations. Power and might are in your hand, and no one can withstand you. Our God, did you not drive out the inhabitants of this land before your people Israel and give it forever to the descendants of Abraham your friend? They have lived in it and have built in it a sanctuary for your Name, saying, 'If calamity comes upon us, whether the sword of judgment, or plague or famine, we will stand in your presence before this temple that bears your Name and will cry out to you in our distress, and you will hear us and save us.' But now here are men from Ammon, Moab and Mount Seir, whose territory you would not allow Israel to invade when they came from Egypt; so they turned away from them and did not destroy them. See how they are repaying us by coming to drive us out of the possession you gave us as an inheritance. Our God, will you not judge them? For we have no power to face this vast army that is attacking us. We do not know what to do, but our eyes are on you." All the men of Judah, with their wives and children and little ones, stood there before the LORD. Then the Spirit of the LORD came on Jahaziel son of Zechariah, the son of Benaiah, the son of Jeiel, the son of Mattaniah, a Levite and descendant of Asaph, as he stood in the assembly. He said: "Listen, King Jehoshaphat and all who live in Judah and Jerusalem! This is what the LORD says to you: 'Do not be afraid or discouraged because of this vast army. For the battle is not yours, but God's. Tomorrow march down against them. They will be climbing up

> by the Pass of Ziz, and you will find them at the end of the gorge in the Desert of Jeruel. You will not have to fight this battle. Take up your positions; stand firm and see the deliverance the LORD will give you, Judah and Jerusalem. Do not be afraid; do not be discouraged. Go out to face them tomorrow, and the LORD will be with you.'" Jehoshaphat bowed down with his face to the ground, and all the people of Judah and Jerusalem fell down in worship before the LORD. Then some Levites from the Kohathites and Korahites stood up and praised the LORD, the God of Israel, with a very loud voice. Early in the morning they left for the Desert of Tekoa. As they set out, Jehoshaphat stood and said, "Listen to me, Judah and people of Jerusalem! Have faith in the LORD your God and you will be upheld; have faith in his prophets and you will be successful." After consulting the people, Jehoshaphat appointed men to sing to the LORD and to praise him for the splendor of his holiness as they went out at the head of the army, saying: "Give thanks to the LORD, for his love endures forever." As they began to sing and praise, the LORD set ambushes against the men of Ammon and Moab and Mount Seir who were invading Judah, and they were defeated. (2 Chronicles 20:1-22, NIV)

This is a great example of the church in operation amid intense crisis coming against her. First, we see at the announcement of trouble the people of Judah came together from every municipality in the region to seek help from the Lord. This was not a spontaneous gathering that happened because of the coming trouble but was a result of the regular gathering to seek the Lord before the trouble began. They made the declaration that no matter what calamity came upon them they would stand in the Lord's presence and cry out to Him. The gathering was generational in nature and boldly proclaimed in humility their utter dependence upon the Lord. The prophetic was in full operation as those appointed and accountable within the management of the temple spoke, under the anointing of the Spirit of the Lord, words of wisdom and knowledge that were judged by King Jehoshaphat and confirmed by the people as actually being from the Lord. It was then that the people were led by singers and musicians of the temple to lift up spontaneous, corporate songs of the Lord. The Lord responded by setting up ambushes against the enemy, and they were eventually defeated. This history of Israel has played itself out again and again within the reports we have heard of the underground church in persecuted countries. This is the battle strategy of the end-time church during the Great Tribulation; not by might but by the Spirit of God.[48] Jesus will never give a directive that He does not provide the power to carry out. This is the essence of Him keeping open an un-shuttable door.

Another example is found in Luke 17 and 18. Jesus finishes up his explanation to the Pharisees about the coming of the Kingdom of

[48] Zech. 4:6 "'Not by might nor by power, but by My Spirit,' says the Lord of hosts."

God by describing the time of the Great Tribulation. Immediately following His explanation of the time of trouble that is to come, Jesus goes into a parable prefaced with a stunning statement in light of the coming trouble: "Men always ought to pray and not lose heart." This is a clear connection between the coming persecution and the function of the last days church. How is it that the church will be able to gather and pray during the time of great persecution and tribulation? Jesus said He is holding open a door that no one can shut!

> And shall God not avenge His own elect who cry out day and night to Him, though He bears long with them? I tell you that He will avenge them speedily. Nevertheless, when the Son of Man comes, will He really find faith on the earth? (Luke 18:7-8)

The cry for the avenging of the Lord will be at its height during the Great Tribulation. Jesus makes the promise that He will keep the door of night and day prayer open. When the church functions in this, then God will avenge them speedily. Faith is required to operate in this manner for the prayer meetings during the time of trouble. They will not be personality driven, nor will they be driven by religious piety. Trusting faith alone will be the great motivator for the church at the end of the age to pray night and day.

Jesus prayed a prayer that is traditionally called the model prayer.[49] It is within this prayer that Jesus reveals His passion for the

---

[49] Matt. 6:9-13 "Pray, then, in this way: 'Our Father who is in heaven, hallowed be Your name. Your kingdom come. Your will be done, on earth as it is in heaven. Give

end of the age: "let it be on earth as it is in heaven." Imagine what Jesus had in mind when He prayed this prayer. There is no doubt that He was considering the day and night elements of worship around the throne in heaven and seeing that adoration be released on the earth. It is what motivated Him to cleanse the temple during His ministry.[50] The activity of prayer is paramount to the spiritual warfare that exists against principalities, in heavenly places, and the manifestation of that warfare upon the earth. It is during the Great Tribulation where that warfare must be waged at its highest levels. We are seeing that today with the underground church in Afghanistan and Iran. How can they pray under threat of rape and death? Jesus is holding open a door.

Let's consider the clear declaration of scripture that all of Israel shall be saved.[51] Isaiah 62 links the continuous night and day prayer through the end of the age to the salvation of Israel. God begins the prophecy with His abiding commitment to His covenant, declaring for the sake of Zion and Jerusalem He will not hold His peace, nor will he rest, "until her righteousness goes forth as brightness, and her salvation as a lamp that burns."[52] This commitment is a dramatic expression. God will not rest but work day and night to bring Israel to the crowning

---

us this day our daily bread. And forgive us our debts, as we also have forgiven our debtors. And do not lead us into temptation, but deliver us from evil. For Yours is the kingdom and the power and the glory forever. Amen.'"

[50] Matt. 21:12-17; John 2:13-16

[51] Rom. 11:26-27 " And so all Israel will be saved, as it is written: 'The Deliverer will come out of Zion, And He will turn away ungodliness from Jacob; for this is My covenant with them, when I take away their sins.'"

[52] Isa. 62:1

glory of the earth. He goes as far as to rename her Hephzibah[53] and the land Beulah.[54] God then describes the partnership that He has made with the watchmen of Israel:

> I have set watchmen [intercessors] on your walls, O Jerusalem; they shall never hold their peace, day or night. You who make mention of the Lord, do not keep silent, and give Him no rest till He establishes and till He makes Jerusalem a praise in the earth. (Isaiah 62:6-7)

This is the main reason why Jesus will hold open the door for night and day prayer. No one can shut this door because God has made a covenant with Himself, that His commitment to Abraham is still true today—there will not be national blessing on the earth unless it is through Abraham's family. God has called forth the end-time church to give Him no rest regarding the end-time promises concerning Israel. Jesus will be the door keeper of that promise. Israel will be saved through the intercession of the church praying day and night at the height of the coming future persecution when Israel will have the veil removed.

> And He will destroy on this mountain the surface of the covering cast over all people, and the veil that is spread over all nations. He will swallow up death forever, and the Lord God will wipe away tears from all faces; the rebuke of His people He

[53] My delight is in her
[54] To marry, posses, own

will take away from all the earth; for the Lord has spoken. And it will be said in that day: "Behold, this is our God; we have waited for Him, and He will save us. This is the Lord; we have waited for Him; we will be glad and rejoice in His salvation." (Isaiah 26:7-9)

CHAPTER SEVEN

The Open Door of Easy Evangelism

Revelation chapter 7 gives us a glimpse of what the great harvest at the end of the age will look like. Immediately after the rapture of the church, putting an end to the rage of Satan, John sees a new scene in heaven. He describes a great multitude of people which no one could number from all nations, tribes, peoples and languages, all standing before the throne of the Lamb. He is fascinated with their dress of white robes and the waving of palm branches.[55] Although the symbolism was very well known in John's era, it is the song that releases the true meaning of their victory. "Salvation belongs to our God who sits on the throne, and to the Lamb!" (Revelation 9-10).

---

[55] In ancient Roman culture the white robe (toga in Latin) was a garment of peace while the palm was a symbol of victory. It was worn by the victor to mark the laying down of arms and the cessation of war.

Then one of the elders gives John the answer to a rhetorical question that he had no capacity to answer. The elder tells John that these are they who have come out of the Great Tribulation, washed their robes, and made them white in the blood of the Lamb.[56] This descriptive answer is telling John that there will be a tremendous ingathering of people touched by the gospel during the time of the Great Tribulation. The open door of evangelism at the end of the age will be not only un-shuttable but unstoppable. It will reach all nations, and they will respond to the Lord's call in the midst of the greatest time of intense persecution.

There is a prophetic picture of the last days evangelism movement shown in John 21. The disciples were in great distress after the crucifixion and resurrection of Jesus. We are not exactly sure when in proximity to the empty tomb that this event happened, but John simply states that some of the disciples were together in one place. He does not discuss what they were saying to each other, nor what their demeanor was. However, there was one simple statement from Simon Peter, wrought with exasperation and disappointment: "I'm going to fish." The inference here is that there was nothing else to do but something familiar that would give immediate results and quell his dissatisfaction with his situation. But as so often happens with fishermen, it did not deliver the results he was hoping for. The all-night

[56] Isa. 1:16-18 "Wash yourselves, make yourselves clean . . . Though your sins are like scarlet, they shall be as white as snow; though they are red like crimson, they shall be as wool."

toil had produced nothing. When morning came, there was a man at the shore that shouted out to them, “Young lads, did you catch anything to eat?” as though a passing traveler wanting to purchase some of their fish. They responded with a simple and dejected “no.” It is then that the story takes on a very unusual turn:

> And He said to them, "Cast the net on the right side of the boat, and you will find some." So they cast, and now they were not able to draw it in because of the multitude of fish. Therefore that disciple whom Jesus loved said to Peter, "It is the Lord!" Now when Simon Peter heard that it was the Lord, he put on his outer garment (for he had removed it), and plunged into the sea. But the other disciples came in the little boat (for they were not far from land, but about two hundred cubits), dragging the net with fish. Then, as soon as they had come to land, they saw a fire of coals there, and fish laid on it, and bread. Jesus said to them, "Bring some of the fish which you have just caught." Simon Peter went up and dragged the net to land, full of large fish, one hundred and fifty-three; and although there were so many, the net was not broken. (John 21:6-11)

It is here that we must go back about three and a half years in time and consider Luke 5 to understand the significance of this prophetic picture:

> So it was, as the multitude pressed about Him to hear the word of God, that He stood by the Lake of Gennesaret, and saw two

> boats standing by the lake; but the fishermen had gone from them and were washing their nets. Then He got into one of the boats, which was Simon's, and asked him to put out a little from the land. And He sat down and taught the multitudes from the boat. When He had stopped speaking, He said to Simon, "Launch out into the deep and let down your nets for a catch." But Simon answered and said to Him, "Master, we have toiled all night and caught nothing; nevertheless at Your word I will let down the net." And when they had done this, they caught a great number of fish, and their net was breaking. So they signaled to their partners in the other boat to come and help them. And they came and filled both the boats, so that they began to sink. (Luke 5:1-7)

There are several points to be made in these two stories concerning evangelism. At the end of Jesus' earthly ministry, when all seemed lost, He brought the disciples back to the time of their original calling. And although there are similarities in the two, there are striking differences that speak to us today. The story at the beginning of their calling was in the midst of the gospel being preached, when the disciples, specifically Peter, had no capacity for faith in Jesus. But this itinerant, rabbinical stranger gives them an outrageous directive: "Launch out into the deep and let down your nets for a catch."

Not only was it outrageous for a rabbi to tell fishermen how to do their job, but the instruction was ridiculous. They had already worked all night and had come up empty. Nevertheless, out of respect, Peter obeyed with no expectation of a catch. He was unprepared for what he would receive. He was so unprepared that he did not bother bringing more nets with him. The one net he had began to break, and the boats began to sink. It was out of this experience that Peter began to follow Jesus. Three and a half years later,[57] Peter found himself in the same situation as the beginning of his calling: out on a boat on the Sea of Galilee, fishing. Once again, a stranger makes outrageous and ridiculous directives, "throw the nets on the other side of the boat." John does not record any argument or emotional response from Peter at that moment. They gave the request their full obedience, even though the request made no sense. What difference does the right side of the boat have to do with the left side? However, as we will see, obedience is mastered within the outrageous, for as they obeyed, the result was overwhelming as a great number of fish filled the nets; 153 to be exact.[58]

The multitude in heaven signifies a tremendous "catch" of people with the gospel during the greatest trial ever on the face of the earth, and obedience will be its greatest lure. The gospel witness will be at its most effective at the most turbulent. It will make no logical sense

---

[57] Although we will not discuss it in this book, consider that the Great Tribulation will begin 3 ½ years after the start of Daniel's 70th week prophecy. (cf. Daniel 9:27; Matt. 24:15-22)

[58] Some commentators have said that the number 153 represents all the nations of the world touched by the Holy Spirit. In Acts 2 there are 17 nations listed as being present during the outpouring at Pentecost. When the sequence of numbers from 1 to 17 are added up it equals 153.

for there to be a countless number of evangelists preaching the gospel when to do so would mean to lose one's life; however, even under the threats of evil men, obedience will be the key. It will not be merely logical obedience but radical obedience to preach a radical message. It is not about making the gospel enticing but preaching the gospel entirely. It would have been much more appealing if Jesus shouted from the shore "Hey! It's me Jesus! Come on in, I have some fish and bread!" But Jesus always gives us a different message than what seems to make sense.

The American Church is losing the gospel message. We are trying to make it all about logic. We make promises that you will have a better life, better success, more riches, more blessing, more honor, etc. if you will just follow Him. Although there are great benefits from abstaining from sin, it is not the primary reason to follow Jesus. Christianity has been a philosophy, a morality, a doctrine, and more recently, it has become a political party—to our folly. However, it is none of these. Christianity is about a person that is so captivating, so endearing, so overwhelming, so *other than*! One glimpse of this man and a person is ruined for all other attractions. However, if you were to listen to the most popular ministries today, it seems that Evangelicalism has totally given up on the draw of this message. The church is impressed by the business strategies of the world to the point where the gospel is not enough. It is enough to save a person, but it is not enough to keep a person. From that incorrect assumption, the pursuant finds itself looking for the latest church growth strategies and approaches; the gospel alone is not enough. We have watered down the message to the degree that, instead of proclaiming the saving power of Jesus, pulpits preach the five ways to gain a better life, or the ten ways to hear from God for your future, etc. The biblical message of the gospel that Jesus preached must return to the church. Consider this, Jesus' entire preaching ministry is summed up in one message: "Repent! For the kingdom of God is at hand!" During the time of intense persecution, nobody will care whether women should be in ministry or not, or if the speaking in tongues is the initial physical evidence for Holy Spirit baptism, or if you are an Arminian or a Calvinist. The church will no longer have the privilege to argue these points when the gospel of Jesus becomes a matter of life and death. The message that Jesus preached will be the most effective message during the Great Tribulation: that is, "People get ready! Jesus is coming! Maranatha!"

Jesus holds open the door of easy evangelism if we share His message. The persecuted church all over the world is not preaching an American gospel; they are preaching a Jesus gospel, a gospel that says you must lose your life to find it.[59] It is the gospel that produces followers that do not love their lives even unto death.[60] The open door of easy evangelism is not that it will be simple for people to be saved,

---

[59] Matt. 10:39 "Whoever finds their life will lose it, and whoever loses their life for my sake will find it."
[60] Rev. 12:11 (NLT) "And they did not love their lives so much that they were afraid to die."

but the open door will make it easier for the messengers to preach the true gospel of the Bible.

> And He said to them, "Go into all the world and preach the gospel to every creature. He who believes and is baptized will be saved; but he who does not believe will be condemned. And these signs will follow those who believe: In My name they will cast out demons; they will speak with new tongues; they will take up serpents; and if they drink anything deadly, it will by no means hurt them; they will lay hands on the sick, and they will recover." So then, after the Lord had spoken to them, He was received up into heaven, and sat down at the right hand of God. And they went out and preached everywhere, the Lord working with them and confirming the word through the accompanying signs. Amen. (Mark 16:15-20)

CHAPTER EIGHT

The Open Door of Biblical Prophetic Revelation

The priest and the prophet have erred through intoxicating drink, they are swallowed up by wine, they are out of the way through intoxicating drink; they err in vision, they stumble in judgment. For all tables are full of vomit and filth; no place is clean. "Whom will he teach knowledge? And whom will he make to understand the message? Those just weaned from milk? Those just drawn from the breasts? For precept must be upon precept, precept upon precept, line upon line, line upon line, here a little, there a little." For with stammering lips and another tongue He will speak to this people. (Isaiah 28:8-11)

I have had a unique history with the church and its many movements in the twilight of the twentieth century. I grew up as a child in the Pentecostal/Charismatic movement through the strict biblical teachings of the Assemblies of God regarding the gift of tongues in the '70s. This was also the height of the Jesus People and the Catholic Charismatic movement, both of which the church I attended was involved in. I continued through my teenage years witnessing the era of the Word of Faith Movement in the '80s and the Toronto Blessing and Brownsville Revival of the '90s. And finally in the 2000s, I have spent the bulk of my adult ministry years watching and participating in, to one degree or another, the fruit of the Vineyard Movement (The Call, IHOP-KC). Most recently, I have been involved with and participating in the Messianic Movement with Dan and Ben Juster and Tikkun America.

Considering this rare but unique history over the last four decades (now beginning my fifth), I feel qualified to speak with both emotion and perception concerning the Holy Spirit and His partnership with the church approaching the last days. This third door will require a close and careful look at the scriptures regarding the importance of the Holy Spirit's role within the last days church.

Isaiah 28 is the coda of the chapters of the Little Apocalypse. It is designed to be a warning. There was an indictment set forth upon the priest and the prophets of Isaiah's day that we should pay attention to: "The priest and the prophet have erred through intoxicating drink, they are swallowed up by wine, they are out of the way through intoxicating drink; they err in vision, they stumble in judgment. For all tables are full of vomit and filth; no place is clean" (Isaiah 28:7-8).

There is a serious indiscretion perpetrated by these ministries of Isaiah's day. The intoxicating drink has overcome them, causing them to err and stumble in both vision and judgment. Verse eight gives the distinct result of this intoxication: vomit and excrement. This is not a one-time indiscretion but a description of the result of this intoxication expressed within the ministry. They are still prophesying with confidence, but it is mixed with pride of self-declared infallibility. As prophets they are trained to speak from the place of the overflow of the Holy Spirit, or in this case, speaking out from what has consumed them. These prophets are operating in their own strength fueled by their own desires. They seem to have no idea that they are in the wrong in the absence of accountability. The priests and the prophets are working together in their transgressions rather than holding each other accountable. The use of drunkenness in the Bible usually refers to mockery, haziness, and distorted vision. This always leads to error. Even more grievous is when it refers to the condition of those speaking on behalf of the Lord.[61]

Not only are those that claim a prophetic spirit speaking out of their own desires, but they are deriding those who attempt to correct their so-called prophetic words using the scriptures. This is how Isaiah

---

[61] This makes the old Pentecostal term "drunk in the Holy Spirit" especially challenging to justify its use.

described the mocking and prideful sayings of the prophet when challenged:

> "Who is it he is trying to teach? To whom is he explaining the message? What are we children just weaned from milk? Infants removed from the breast? For precept must be upon precept, precept upon precept, line upon line, line upon line, here a little, there a little.". . . So the Lord's word to them will sound like meaningless gibberish, senseless babbling, a syllable here, a syllable there. As a result, they will fall on their backsides when they try to walk, and be injured, ensnared, and captured. (Isaiah 28:9-13)

The prophet being corrected is asking the question, "Who do they think they are talking to? Little children?" signifying the disdain he has for the questioning of his prophetic word. He then goes on to say of the challenge, "We've heard before, over and over again, this rule and that rule, this scripture and that scripture…" This passage from Isaiah 28:10 has been used out of context for years. It was always brought up as a proof text in how to study the scriptures. However, in true context, we see that it is actually used as a mockery by those that place prophetic words equal to the scriptures—such as the "Word of Faith" argument pitting Rhema against Logos when they are essentially the same Greek word. As a matter of fact, one would think that the manifestation of the Spirit in the ministry gift of the "word of wisdom" and the "word of knowledge" in 1 Corinthians 12 would make use of the word Rhema as being a "now" word of the Lord, placing by default the scriptures as a "then" word of the Lord with all of its staleness. However, the Greek word used in "word of wisdom" and "word of knowledge" is Logos which then would change that particular manifestation of the Holy Spirit into a prophetic scriptural expression rather than an expression of the prophet as it is so often cited as justification for that type of ministry.

My point is not to argue the terms but to argue the use. In the last days, the prophetic ministry of the Holy Spirit will be a necessary function of the Trinitarian ministry which has a great danger of being abused and actually used by Satan to cause discouragement and confusion due to lack of knowledge and understanding. The church must turn away from this and recognize the purpose of Jesus sending us the Comforter. We find that in Joel 2 and John 14:

> And it shall come to pass afterward That I will pour out My Spirit on all flesh; your sons and your daughters shall prophesy, your old men shall dream dreams, your young men shall see visions. And also on My menservants and on My maidservants I will pour out My Spirit in those days. (Joel 2:28-29)
>
> But the comforter, the Holy Spirit, whom the Father will send in My name, He will teach you all things, and bring to your

> remembrance all things that I said to you [in scripture]. (John 14:26)[62]

The great need of our day will be the scriptural stewardship of the last days prophetic pouring out of the Spirit. It will take a generation of *elders* to help steward rightly this outpouring on our sons and daughters. Consider the verses that precede this prophecy, as it is all in the same context:

> Consecrate a fast, call a sacred assembly; gather the people [to pray], sanctify the congregation [for worship], assemble the elders [for accountability], gather the children and nursing babes [to teach them]. (Joel 2:15-16)[63]

The end-time pouring out of the Spirit will require the stewardship of the local church to keep it solid in the Word. We must remember that although we are to test every spirit, our first response is to NOT believe every spirit.[64] We are to have a healthy skepticism of any prophetic word that we hear until it can be examined. There is only ONE measure of the prophetic by which we can hold any word to as if it is from God:

---

[62] Bracketed phrase mine

[63] Bracketed phrase mine

[64] 1 John 4:1 "Beloved, do not believe every spirit, but test the spirits, whether they are of God." The Greek word for "test" is "dokimazo" meaning to scrutinize; to recognize as genuine after examination.

> All Scripture is given by inspiration of God, and is useful for teaching, reproof,[65] correction and training in righteousness, so that the servant of God may be thoroughly equipped for every good work. (2 Timothy 3:16-17)

In 2020, our nation went through a very challenging time (and as of the writing of this, the challenge is still growing). During this time, the church faced a greater challenge than that of the time since the 9/11 attacks. Most of the controversy orbited around the prophetic ministry regarding Covid-19, racism, and politics. The prophetic ministry around these subjects proved that it had a weakness and a flaw within the understanding and function of this important biblical church expression. Prophetic words were being declared and received as flawless, inspired, and to be adhered to without proper judgment of the scriptures or seeking wisdom of the Spirit and accountability of church leaders. With the aid of social media, the battle lines were drawn, and the war began among the saints; a so-called prophet said one thing, and another said something else. Dates were set for the ending of the pandemic, and even an invasion by China was predicted, as if it was from the Lord. These unaccountable or self-accountable prophets were releasing prophecies that were trumpeted across the internet at lightning speed from all over the world; they were made YouTube stars and launched podcasts and webinars featuring the latest group of prophets and their continuous words of presumption. But when those prophecies

[65] Gr. *elegchos*: a proof, that by which a thing is proved or tested

did not come to pass, there was mostly silence except for those that refused to accept their error and the small handful of those that repented. An even smaller group of those in godly humility announced that they would cease prophesying altogether. The scripture is clear that New Testament prophetic ministry is not a perfect ministry by design, and so must be judged against the scriptures and under accountability of the leadership of a local congregation that the person giving the prophetic word is an active part of. I see no exception to this rule.

> For we know in part and we prophesy in part. But when that which is perfect has come, then that which is in part will be done away. When I was a child, I spoke as a child, I understood as a child, I thought as a child; but when I became a man, I put away childish things. For now we see in a mirror, dimly, but then face to face. Now I know in part, but then I shall know just as I also am known. (1 Corinthians 13:9-12)

In 2020, the primary measure of the prophetic words distributed by social media around the world and the confidence of those words was not through scripture but through the so-called accuracy of past prophecies. In other words, if the "prophet" was shown to be accurate in the past, then what they say in the future should be considered carte blanche, as if coming from God. There is absolutely no scriptural stipulation for that allowance. We are not to accept any prophetic word regardless of the so-called track record until it is tested against the scriptures. And if the scriptures cannot be discerned over any prophetic word, then the speaker should remain silent in humility until a proper and reasonable judgment can be ascertained by the speaker's spiritual leaders.

> Let two or three prophets speak, and let the others judge. But if anything is revealed to another who sits by, let the first keep silent. For you can all prophesy one by one, that all may learn and all may be encouraged. And the spirits of the prophets are subject to the prophets. For God is not the author of confusion but of peace. (1 Corinthians 14:29-33)

Personally, I believe that prophetic words should not be a social media disseminating function. It must come from the local church and have the liability of tested and seasoned elders of that church to decide its validity in accordance with the scriptures. From that place there can be confidence through accountability, reproof, correction, and then there can be distribution. The inspiration of those who speak prophetically are in subjugation to the Word of God. The judgment remains in their church community and not in their ministry board or peers. Those who share prophetically cannot be a lone ranger who considers themselves superior to any church or church governing body. Mark Chironna, whom I have known of his ministry since my teenage years, is a respected person in the ministry of the prophetic. He sent a statement over twitter in response to the mangled prophetic ministry:

> When so-called "prophets" carry themselves as if their individual gift makes them superior to others because they have

> a "revelation", they are proving they are *not* truly functioning in the prophetic. Rather, their self-centered demeanor reveals they operate in divination.[66]

I am not discouraged by the current upheaval of the ministry of the prophetic; I am excited that God is choosing this time to reveal our shortcomings and to strengthen this most needed end-time ministry of the Holy Spirit. The open door for biblical prophetic revelation is not for the specialized minister, nor for the office of the prophet, but for everyday believers who make up the majority of the end-time church. It will be the everyday believer that will be faced with the increase in persecution that is to come and will be in need to be encouraged by the prophetic word that they may have received that has been bathed in the Word.

I have in my possession an old book by Pastor Dennis Cramer that was written back in 1981. He has since traveled the world teaching on prophecy to local churches worldwide. Yet while he was still a local pastor of a small congregation in Williamsport, PA, he wrote the following:

> It is a historical fact that the early church, as a whole, operated in the gift of prophecy. That is the early church had a very active laity in terms of being prophetic. It was not just a few strange unapproachable "prophetic types" sitting on mountain tops somewhere, dressed in camel's hair, eating locust and honey,

[66] @markchironna; December 22, 2017.

> and hearing voices. Rather, the entire church body understood the activity of the Holy Spirit as He inspired believers to speak God's prophetic word. The early church approached prophecy as the supernatural manifestation it is, and yet with a very practical application. Prophecy was part of their lives. They believed God's Word concerning prophecy and acted upon it. They were a prophetic people. This same prophetic movement among today's laity is precisely what God is once again restoring. God is not endorsing the "spooky spiritual" types who continue to reinforce misconceptions surrounding prophetic ministry. He is developing a practical, yet powerful Church in these last days. He is raising up an army and a nation to operate in powerful prophetic giftings. The prophetic purpose and plan of God for the Body of Christ is coming to pass in our generation.[67]

It has been forty years since this quote. The church's current status has proven that we are in great need to return to its sentiments. The Lord has promised that He will open the door for the faithful church in the last days and the prophetic ministry will be the front-line agent for the persecuted church. As the Taliban in Afghanistan begins hunting down church groups and leaders, we will hear of the tremendous use of the ministry of the prophetic to rescue and save lives. The days of the prophetic minister standing on a platform

---

[67] Dennis Cramer, *You Can All Prophesy* (Williamsport PA: Arrow Publications, 2003), xvi.

"reading people's mail" and being called a prophet is meaningless and capricious when it comes to persecution and tribulation. In the author's opinion, this form of the prophetic ministry must go the way of the circus act. The end-time church must witness and embrace the use, purpose, and application of the true objective and function of the prophetic ministry. Without it we will be left floundering in a sea of confusion when the Lord pours out His Spirit in the latter days. The Lord is raising up humble and submitted people of God to model with their lives and experience what it means to be prophetic in the midst of persecution.[68] Let me conclude with a shocking and disturbing passage from Zechariah 13:

> On that day a fountain will be opened for the dynasty of David and for the people of Jerusalem, a fountain to cleanse them from all their sins and impurity. "And on that day," says the LORD of Heaven's Armies, "I will erase idol worship throughout the land, so that even the names of the idols will be forgotten. I will remove from the land both the false prophets and the spirit of impurity that came with them. If anyone continues to prophesy, his own father and mother will tell him, 'You must die, for you have prophesied lies in the name of the LORD.' And as he prophesies, his own father and mother will stab him. On that day people will be ashamed to claim the prophetic gift. No one will pretend to be a prophet by wearing prophet's clothes. He

---

[68] Brother Yun of China; Pastor Mario Barroso of Cuba; Pastor Andrew Brunson in Turkey

will say, ‘I’m no prophet; I’m a farmer. I began working for a farmer as a boy.’ And if someone asks, ‘Then what about those wounds on your chest?’ he will say, ‘I was wounded at my friends’ house!’ (Zechariah 13:1-6 NLT)

CHAPTER NINE

The Apostolic Open Doors

In the previous chapters I have expressed the idea that the Lord Jesus will personally hold open a door for the end-time church to not only survive during the Great Tribulation but to thrive as a witness upon the earth until the very end of the age.[69] Although there are probably more doors that I could have highlighted, I have chosen these three as the ones that are in need of training and practice before the birth pangs begin—of which I am convinced is not far ahead of us. I would like to take this chapter to show that these three doors are not just randomly picked. These were the three functions of the first-century church, as

[69] Matt. 28:19-20 "Go therefore and make disciples of all the nations, baptizing them in the name of the Father and of the Son and of the Holy Spirit, teaching them to observe all things that I have commanded you; and lo, I am with you always, even to the end of the age."

shown in the book of Acts, and were all centered around the commanded mission given to the Apostles.

In the prior chapter, I made the argument about the need for Biblical prophetic revelation in the end days connected to the Joel 2 prophecy of the last days pouring out of the Holy Spirit. We as believers have received the Holy Spirit as evidence by our confession of faith in the saving knowledge and Lordship of Jesus,[70] but there is also a promise of strength that the Lord emphasized will come upon all believers that will aid them to maintain steadfastness. It is within the book of Acts that we are given clear definition, function, and application of this end-time release to persevere.

First, we must define what the end-time pouring out of the Holy Spirit is specifically for. Simply but profoundly, it is for the application of power for the mission of the end-time church. Over the many years of my journey there has been a mix of claims of jubilant and extravagant expressions of human beings in the midst of the overflow of joy *attributed* to the Holy Spirit. I have been in hundreds of these meetings. I have always enjoyed the ecstatic expression, and oftentimes participated in them. The Bible does not speak against this at all. On the contrary, there is much in the Word about the need for blissful jubilation of the people of God; but even as great and emotional as it has been, it is not the proof of the presence of the Holy Spirit. Some have claimed

[70] 1 Cor. 12:3 "No one who is speaking by the Spirit of God says, 'Jesus be cursed,' and no one can say, 'Jesus is Lord,' except by the Holy Spirit."

power in discernment, or words of knowledge, and other gifts of the Spirit as the proof of the presence of the Holy Spirit. They are not. Let's look at a brief outline of the function of the Holy Spirit in the life of Jesus. He was active at the conception of Jesus through Mary (Matthew 1:18); He was involved in the growth of Jesus as a young boy (Luke 2:40); He was in full force at Jesus' baptism (Luke 3:21-22); He led Jesus to be tempted (Luke 4:1); Jesus began His ministry in the power of the Spirit (Luke 4:14); and Jesus cast out demons by the Spirit (Matthew 12:28), went to the cross by the Spirit (Hebrews 9:14), and was resurrected by the Spirit (Romans 8:11). Some would like to take this concept and liken it to a subordination within the Divine Trinity as if Jesus was dependent on the Holy Spirit; however, that is not the clear teaching of the scripture concerning the interactive relation of the "echad" of God.[71] God Almighty is not a trinity, rather the Divine Trinity is God Almighty and thus there cannot be any subordination. Jesus is the name given to the conceived human body which the Logos (second person of the Divine Trinity) *"agreed"* to forever abide in a human form as the only begotten Son of the Father. Although He is the provisional atonement needed to cover human beings, this does not change His status in the Divine Godhead. Jesus, the only begotten Son of the Father, is fully Logos abiding as the fully human Jesus functioning with the Holy Spirit within the Divine Godhead. This makes Jesus Christ a very distinctive and exceptional man to ever live

---

[71] Echad is the Hebrew word for One but not as a single digit but within a complexity of unity. The 3 persons of God are co-equal, co-eternal, co-existent.

on the earth, for within Him all the fullness of the Deity exists[72] of which we can never attain, nor should we desire to. For just as Jesus did not feel equality with God was something to be grasped nor should we feel equality with Jesus is something for us to be grasped.

> Have this mind among yourselves, which is yours in Christ Jesus, who, though he was in the form of God, did not count equality with God a thing to be grasped, but emptied himself, by taking the form of a servant, being born in the likeness of men. Being found in human form, he humbled himself by becoming obedient to the point of death, even death on a cross. (Philippians 2:5-8)

Jesus' life is to be emulated and His earthly ministry to be imitated. Jesus' fellowship with the Holy Spirit is evident in that all He did was through direct partnership with the Holy Spirit. While the modern-day charismatic expressions are associated with being the primary ministry of the Holy Spirit, the true ministry of the Holy Spirit is biblically clear. The scriptural and experiential essence of the Holy Spirit is the in-dwelling power of God to be witnesses of Jesus now and in the age to come.[73]

> When the Spirit of truth comes, He will guide you into all truth. For He will not speak on His own, but He will speak what He hears, and He will declare to you what is to come. He will

[72] Col. 2:9 "For in Him dwells all the fullness of the Godhead bodily."
[73] Discipleship of nations will continue into the Millennial Kingdom.

> glorify Me by taking from what is Mine and disclosing it to you. Everything that belongs to the Father is Mine. That is why I said that the Spirit will take from what is Mine and disclose it to you. (John 16:13-15)

Being a witness is the act of making Jesus known which leads us to the one biblical proof of the presence and function of the Holy Spirit that all other expressions must come under, and it is spoken of by Jesus in Acts 1:8: "But you shall receive power when the Holy Spirit has come upon you; and you shall be witnesses of Me in Jerusalem, and in all Judea and Samaria, and to the end of the earth."

The Bible is clear that the Holy Spirit will come upon and fill a person for the expressed need of power to be a witness of Jesus especially in the midst of tribulation. The Greek word for *power* is *dunamis*, which means inherent strength and ability; to be capable and prepared for it to be used. The Greek word for witness is *martus*[74] from whence we get the English word martyr. In the scriptures the word is used for both those that are giving testimony of what they have seen and those that have died for that testimony. In English there is a distinction between the two words, in New Testament Greek there is not. For example:

---

[74] Greek Martus: in a legal and historical sense a spectator of anything; to witness. In an ethical sense: those who have proved the genuineness of their faith in Christ by undergoing a violent death.

(at the trial of Stephen) "They also set up false [martus] who said, 'This man does not cease to speak blasphemous words against this holy place and the law.'" (Acts 6:13)

(Paul's testimony about the death of Stephen) "And when the blood of Your [martus] Stephen was shed, I also was standing by consenting to his death, and guarding the clothes of those who were killing him." (Acts 22:20)

The Greek word *martus* does not imply death as does the English word *martyr.* To be a witness is not simply to be one who gives testimony but to be one who lives within that testimony. The apostles were direct eyewitnesses to the death and resurrection of Jesus; they had the power of the actual experience with them. However, Jesus indicates that relaying an experience is not enough, that it is the power exuded by the Holy Spirit that transforms a debate about Jesus into a declaration for Jesus so that the hearer would be moved and convicted to ask the question as did the hearers in Acts 2, "What shall we do?"[75]

The framework of the ministry of the Holy Spirit is that He will dwell within the believer to empower them for a particular task at a particular time for a particular purpose.[76] It seems obvious that for forty days Jesus had been teaching about the coming kingdom, more than

[75] Acts 2:37 "When the people heard this, they were cut to the heart and said to Peter and the other apostles, 'Brothers, what shall we do?'"
[76] Luke 12:11-12 "When you are brought before synagogues, rulers, and authorities, do not worry about how to defend yourselves or what to
say. For at that time the Holy Spirit will teach you what you should say."

likely expounding on His discourse from the Mount of Olives days before He was crucified. We can conclude this by the nature of the question the disciples asked before He ascended: "Lord, will you at this time restore the [Davidic] kingdom to Israel?" (Acts 1:6). Jesus answers them by instructing them on one more task that is to be performed. He tells them that they must be His witnesses and be the agents to gather back the elect of God. We can surmise that the seemingly delay of the Messianic Hope coming is so that the disciples can go locally, regionally, and globally as witnesses to the fact that Jesus is the long-awaited Messiah; and though He was crucified, He rose from the dead and is returning to the earth to establish the kingdom of God in Jerusalem. This would have been the only way the disciples could have understood the message of the promised outpouring of the Holy Spirit.[77] They would not have thought that the Holy Spirit would make their church meetings better or their crusades livelier. There was only one framework built around the waiting for power: being a martus by laying down their lives for the sake of the task.

This was the permeating message of the Azusa Street outpouring[78] at the turn of the last century that was signified by signs and wonders, specifically the speaking of tongues. They believed that the sign associated with speaking in other tongues was a repeat of Acts

---

[77] It is interesting to note that just before the outpouring of the Holy Spirit in Acts, Jesus and the disciples were discussing the coming of the kingdom of God. Just after His ascension, the two men in white apparel made the statement of His return. The message of the power of the Holy Spirit is book ended by the end-time message.
[78] The Azusa Street Revival took place in Los Angeles, California on April 9, 1906.

2 and that the return of Jesus was soon. The glossolalia (speaking the divine language) would also be accompanied by xenoglossy (speaking a natural language previously unknown to the speaker)[79] and was also considered to indicate to which country they would bring the gospel.[80] Something similar was seen again amongst the Jesus Movement of the late 1960s and early 1970s, which was partly a reaction against the free-love counterculture from which it originated. The charismatic movement had already been in full swing for about a couple of decades when this movement broke out. The theology of the Jesus Movement also called for a return to simple living and frugality. The Jesus People had a strong belief in miracles, signs and wonders, faith, healing, prayer, the Bible, and powerful works of the Holy Spirit.[81] The movement tended towards strong evangelism and millennialism. Some of the most-read books by those within the movement included Ron Sider's *Rich Christians in an Age of Hunger* and Hal Lindsey's *The Late Great Planet Earth*.[82]

Messianic Judaism is intertwined with the Jesus Movement of the 1960s. During that revival, many young people with strong, ethnically Jewish backgrounds came to faith in Yeshua. Societal

---

[79] David Swincer, *Tongues: Genuine Biblical Languages—A Careful Construct of the Nature, Purpose, and Operation of the Gift of Tongues for the Church* (South Australia: Integrity Publications, 2016), 88–90.
[80] William D. Faupel. *Glossolalia as Foreign Language: An Investigation of the Twentieth-Century Pentecostal Claim*. "Archived copy"Archived from the original on 29 April 2005. Retrieved 27 April 2005.
[81] David J. Gyertson. *One Divine Moment*. (Bristol House, Limited, 1995).
[82] Larry Eskridge, "Jesus People" in Erwin Fahlbusch, Geoffrey William Bromiley, David B. Barrett, *Encyclopedia of Christianity*.

changes of that time offered these young Jewish people the freedom to maintain their Jewish heritage while embracing faith in Jesus as their promised Messiah. The attitude shifted from, "We are Christians who happen to be Jewish," to, "We are Jews who believe in Jesus." This represented a new mindset that shaped the modern movement of Messianic Judaism.[83, 84]

There is a clear historical line that has been drawn from the primitive church in the book of Acts to modernity. It has only been in the last thirty years that we have seen a decline in the emphasis of the power of the Spirit used for evangelism and an increase in its personal use for power, popularity, self-help purposes, and financial prosperity. Biblical Spirit empowerment has everything to do with the liberation of the soul through the gospel, which also includes the priority of prayer and the use of the prophetic gifts of the Spirit. These three together form the framework for the movement of the early church, a church that had the reputation for turning the world upside down and was firmly ensconced within the three doors that no man can shut. [85]

It is of no coincidence that Peter, the one who denied Jesus, was to be the one to preach the first message of the church. His own

---

[83]"History of Messianic Judaism," Jewish Voice, June 19, 2018, https://www.jewishvoice.org/read/blog/history-messianic-judaism.

[84] The Messianic movement is centered around the gospel brought to the Jew first in anticipation for the time of the end when all of Israel will be saved. The movement involves the pouring out of the Holy Spirit to bring the gospel in power to Israel.

[85] Acts 17:6 "But when they did not find them, they dragged Jason and some brethren to the rulers of the city, crying out, 'These who have turned the world upside down have come here too.'"

personal witness was wrought with betrayal, pride, and doubt. But when finally confronted with the power of the Spirit, he is the one that stands up with all boldness and preaches the first gospel message, rooted in eschatology with great effectiveness. Peter was timid and defeated; Jesus called a prayer meeting for ten days; the Holy Spirit was given with power; Peter spoke with boldness the oracles of God. The three doors of prayer, prophetic revelation, and evangelism are on full display.

We see another example of the three doors in Acts, chapters 3 and 4. Peter and John approach the temple gates and are confronted by a man whom they have seen before. He was lame and asking for alms of which was his practice daily. Peter would have passed this man hundreds of times when he would visit the temple. Nevertheless, this time there was a prophetic revelation that was released in his spirit. Peter fixes his eyes on the man and makes a declaration to him and commands him to walk in the name of Jesus of Nazareth. The man is strengthened and totally healed and draws a crowd. Peter and John used this opportunity to share the gospel, preaching as witnesses of Jesus, and about 5000 men heard and came into belief in the Messiah. As a result, Peter and John were placed in jail overnight. When asked by what authority they had been speaking, Peter is then described as being filled with the Holy Spirit and spoke to them through the power of the Spirit:

> Rulers of the people and elders of Israel: If we this day are judged for a good deed done to a helpless man, by what means he has been made well, let it be known to you all, and to all the people of Israel, that by the name of Jesus Christ of Nazareth, whom you crucified, whom God raised from the dead, by Him this man stands here before you whole. This is the 'stone which was rejected by you builders, which has become the chief cornerstone.' Nor is there salvation in any other, for there is no other name under heaven given among men by which we must be saved. (Acts 4:8-12)

The message Peter speaks as a martus was seen as boldness by his audience. The miracle of the lame man was done to increase the weight of the witness. The only response the authorities had was to threaten them with physical violence as when they were first arrested. Peter and John, though, remained undeterred until they reached their companions and explained to them the events that transpired. It was then that they instinctively went into a prayer meeting and prophesied the Word of God over their situation, and once again, we see the activation of the three open doors: prayer, evangelism, and prophetic revelation.

> "Now, Lord, look on their threats, and grant to Your servants that with all boldness they may speak Your word, by stretching out Your hand to heal, and that signs and wonders may be done through the name of Your holy Servant Jesus." And when they

> had prayed, the place where they were assembled together was shaken; and they were all filled with the Holy Spirit, and they spoke the word of God with boldness. (Acts 4:29-31)

In Acts 5, we see more preaching apostles seized and thrown into prison. At night, it is reported that an angel of the Lord came and opened the prison doors to bring them out of the jail. The next part of the story should be that they ran to safety, but instead the angel told them to go stand in the temple and preach again. The next morning, when the greatest number of people would be at the temple, the newly released apostles began to preach Jesus. They were once again apprehended and brought before the council. When they were told that they are not to preach, they began preaching to the council, emphasizing: "We are His witnesses to these things, and so also is the Holy Spirit whom God has given to those who obey Him" (Acts 5:32).

The council had them beaten and commanded that they ought not speak in the name of Jesus, and they were released. Upon their return to their homes, the scriptures record this response: "So, they departed from the presence of the council, rejoicing that they were counted worthy to suffer shame for His name. And daily in the temple, and in every house, they did not cease teaching and preaching Jesus as the Christ" (Acts 5:41-42). We continue to see time and time again the activity of the three doors of night and day prayer, evangelism, and the prophetic in operation.

There is one more jump I would like to take within the narrative of Acts. This took place about ten years after Acts 2—a story about a man named Cornelius; not just a random man but a Gentile and an officer in the Roman army. It seems that within the ten years of the disciples being witnesses, it had reached Caesarea and created secret believers—even in the Roman guard. As the story continues, we see the first door of night and day prayer come into view:

> There was a certain man in Caesarea called Cornelius, a centurion of what was called the Italian Regiment, a devout man and one who feared God with all his household, who gave alms generously to the people, and prayed to God always. About the ninth hour of the day[86] he saw clearly in a vision an angel of God coming in and saying to him, "Cornelius!" And when he observed him, he was afraid, and said, "What is it, lord?" So he said to him, "Your prayers and your alms have come up for a memorial before God." (Acts 10:1-4)

Cornelius was visited with a vision of an angel delivering a message for him to send men and go and collect Peter who was lodging in Joppa (Tel-Aviv today). The next day we see Peter praying the minchah[87] when it was interrupted by two servants and a Roman

---

[86] Jews are required to pray three times daily: in the morning, in the afternoon, and at nightfall. These prayers are called morning prayer (*shacharit*), afternoon prayer (*minchah*), and evening prayer (*arvith* or *maariv*). The ninth hour was 3 p.m. https://www.chabad.org/library/article_cdo/aid/682091/jewish/The-Three-Daily-Prayers.htm

[87] The sixth hour was at about noon.

soldier. Peter, expecting to be arrested and beaten, had been in this situation many times over the decade of being a witness. He was probably already making his getaway plan. It was then that the Spirit spoke to him and confirmed that they are part of the plan of God. After hearing of who summoned him, Peter agreed to travel back with them to see Cornelius. It is here that we see once again the end-time doors. Upon Peter's arrival, Cornelius had gathered together relatives and close friends to be a part of this event. Cornelius tells Peter how he was fasting and praying, as was the custom of devotion for the Jewish God. He then explained to him that in prayer he had a vision and was told that a man named Peter was lodging nearby and that this man would have a message that Cornelius needed to hear. This is a picture of the door of easy evangelism. You would think that Peter, feeling the pressure, would want to come up with something that would really impress them. But, as we see, Peter did not have to seek for a prophetic word to give Cornelius, nor did he speak in riddles or with ambiguity of what the Lord wanted to say to his host; Peter did not "read his mail." There was absolutely no hesitation by Peter to bring forth the message that he was to speak:

> Then Peter opened his mouth and said: "In truth I perceive that God shows no partiality. But in every nation whoever fears Him and works righteousness is accepted by Him. The word which God sent to the children of Israel, preaching peace through Jesus Christ—He is Lord of all—that word you know, which was

> proclaimed throughout all Judea, and began from Galilee after the baptism which John preached: how God anointed Jesus of Nazareth with the Holy Spirit and with power, who went about doing good and healing all who were oppressed by the devil, for God was with Him. (Acts 10:34-38)

Peter was saying that Cornelius already knew of the message that had been preached the past ten years, which is why he had shown devotion to God in alms, prayers, and fasting. But the new information of which Peter was a witness to (martus) is that Jesus, who is resurrected, will judge the living and the dead. Peter continues:

> And we are witnesses of all things which He did both in the land of the Jews and in Jerusalem, whom they killed by hanging on a tree. Him, God raised up on the third day, and showed Him openly, not to all the people, but to witnesses chosen before by God, even to us who ate and drank with Him after He arose from the dead. And He commanded us to preach to the people, and to testify that it is He who was ordained by God to be Judge of the living and the dead. To Him all the prophets witness that, through His name, whoever believes in Him will receive remission of sins." (Acts 10:39-43)

Peter framed the message of salvation around eschatology and gave witness to the death, resurrection, and the judgment at the end of the age. While Peter was still speaking, the Holy Spirit poured out on Cornelius and his entire family, and they began to speak with tongues the magnificence of God. The three doors in operation seen here are evident: night and day prayer, easy evangelism, and biblical prophetic revelation around a framework of the last days.

This was the continuous function of the early church; they were consumed with the return of Jesus, convinced of that fact by His death and resurrection. Although they were first in church history, they acted as an end-times ministry. They had no expectation of a 2000-year church history; they had no expectation of Jesus delaying His return. They operated from a place of the filling of the Holy Spirit, enabling operational boldness. Imagine what the church would look like if we paused all our programs and all of our self-help groups and took one year to focus on operating within the open doors of Revelation 3:8. What if the Holy Spirit made it perfectly clear that this was His desire for us to do? Could we even do it at this point? We have taken the better part of two years chasing Covid, Trump, and BLM, while the Spirit waits. We have been concerned with masks, vaccines, and American rights, while the Spirit waits. We are afraid of gospel preaching, signs, wonders, and healings, while the Spirit waits. What is He waiting for, you may ask? He is waiting for the church to put Jesus on display as the early church did. It is not about making Him popular; it is not about making Him palatable; it is about demonstrating Him with provability.

There are great days ahead of us. There are terrible days ahead of us. The world looks at us as weak, troubled people. They are not impressed with the underground church in Afghanistan holding the line and keeping strong His name. The world would end up blaming them, as they consider it a holy war between two religions. But the world has no say and no sway in the life of the redeemed of the Lord. Jesus would say to the underground church the same thing He said to the church in Philadelphia:

"I see your works; I see what's going on and vengeance is mine. There will be a day of reckoning. I hold the key of David, I will open the doors that no man can shut. Just hold fast to My name even unto death, keep My Word even unto death, and pray the Holy Spirit to come and empower you to be witnesses of my name! You will not be denied! Behold, I am coming quickly! Hold fast to what you have so that no one may take your crown!"

We need a drastic change; we need a definite turnaround! We need to stop trying to get the church to look like America and need to lead the church to look like Jesus—not the Caucasian, hippie Jesus with blue eyes and not even the roaring lion. We need to look like the slain Lamb of God who sits on the throne. That is our confidence. We follow a slain lamb, not a roaring lion.[88] Our confidence is not in the persona of power but in the persona of meekness. It is not the victory of the lion

---

[88] Rev. 5:4-6 "So I wept much, because no one was found worthy to open and read the scroll, or to look at it. But one of the elders said to me, 'Do not weep. Behold, the Lion of the tribe of Judah, the Root of David, has prevailed to open the scroll and to loose its seven seals.' And I looked, and behold, in the midst of the throne and of the four living creatures, and in the midst of the elders, stood a Lamb as though it had been slain."

that will grant us success but the sufferings of the lamb slain from the foundation of the world.[89]

[89] Rev. 13:8 ". . . the Book of life of the Lamb, slain from the foundation of the world."

CHAPTER TEN

Beyond the Open Doors

I have attempted to point out how Revelation 3:7-13 is a clear directive from the Holy Spirit concerning the end-time church and its priorities to be victorious during the greatest time of persecution. The scriptures are clear that Jesus will return at a time that the Father has set by His own authority and sovereignty. This is the blessed hope that we are waiting for: the Bridegroom is coming and a new age is about to be birthed! However, with that holy expectation there must be a holy preparation. Every bride prepares herself for her nuptials. Every mother prepares for the coming newborn. We would deem them both immature and irresponsible if there was no preparation for these two life-altering events. How absurd would it be then to counsel people that there is nothing you must do but wait for the "any moment" rapture to just happen some day.

If there is anything that the "little apocalypse" of Isaiah and the letters of Jesus to the seven churches found in the book of Revelation tell us is that we must prepare. Not only in those chapters are we given the sense of the need for readiness, but it is an overarching and emphasized theme throughout the entirety of the holy scriptures.

> Finally, be strong in the Lord and in his mighty power. Put on the full armor of God, so that you can take your stand against the devil's schemes. For our struggle is not against flesh and blood, but against the rulers, against the authorities, against the powers of this dark world and against the spiritual forces of evil in the heavenly realms. Therefore put on the full armor of God, so that when the day of evil comes, you may be able to stand your ground, and after you have done everything, to stand. Stand firm. (Ephesians 6:10-14, NIV)

When searching for a title to this book, my deepest memories brought up the title to a song that my siblings and I sang when we used to tour local churches as a gospel musical group, some thirty years ago. It was originally performed by the Gaither Vocal Band, called "Beyond the Open Door."[90]

---

[90] Shawn Craig: Beyond The Open Door, Capitol CMG Publishing, © 1990 Star Song Music

> Hear the spirit calling to wake the living dead,
> To reach the huddled masses who cry out for living bread.
> Arise oh mighty army, take up thy shield and sword
> For the Father lifts His golden lamp beside the open door.
>
> Beyond the open door is a new and fresh anointing,
> Hear the Spirit calling you to go.
> Walk on through the door for the Lord will go before you
> Into a greater power you've never known before

All these years later from the singing of that song, those words never had more importance than they do in the age we are living. The opportunity for the victorious church as the Bride of Christ is at hand. However, before we will see the fruits of victory, we need to be in the battle, and as in every battle plan, there is always a clear path to victory. The final door that the Lord is calling the end-time church to walk through is the door of the way of escape. It is not escape from the battle but escape from defeat.

> No trial has overtaken you that is not faced by others. And God is faithful: He will not let you be tried beyond what you are able to bear, but with the trial will also provide a way out so that you may be able to endure it. (1 Corinthians 10:13)

Some may read this book and conclude that I am giving a scenario of the church defeated and weak. Others may say God would not allow us to suffer. The biggest problem with that line of thinking is that we are all observing—in real time—a great persecution of our brothers and sisters all over the world. But this is nothing new. In 2017, Open Doors Ministries released an analysis of persecution trends over the past quarter-century. The top ten nations with the most persecution of Christianity over a twenty-five-year span were: North Korea, Saudi Arabia, Iran, Somalia, Afghanistan, Maldives, Yemen, Sudan, Vietnam, and China.[91]

The argument on whether the church is called to face suffering is not a question at all for the majority of Christians around the world. We in the American Church hold to our cozy doctrine of escapism while secretly and quietly knowing full well that we are not immune to trouble and crisis happening in America before the return of Jesus.

The Bible inexplicably teaches that God's elect, the Bride of Christ, will face the Great Tribulation through the representatives of Satan described as the Antichrist and the false prophet. There is a growing rejection of pan-millennialism: the tongue in cheek position of just waiting till it happens and see how it all pans out. Although it is somewhat *cute* in its explanation, this attitude will turn out to be consequential concerning the biblical command of preparedness. The position that this author takes, regarding the end-time drama, is referred to as Historic PreMillennialism Pre-wrath. I would encourage you to

---

[91] "The 50 Countries Where It's Most Dangerous to Follow Jesus in 2021," Christianity Today, January 13, 2021.
https://www.christianitytoday.com/news/2021/january/christian-persecution-2021-countries-open-doors-watch-list.html

search out the position yourself, and I highly recommend the easily readable paperback titled: *Prewrath: A Very Short Introduction to the Great Tribulation, Rapture, and Day of the Lord* by Alan E Kurchner.[92] Here is an excerpt:

> Some may question why a book on Christ's return is necessary. They may say, "What only matters is that Jesus is returning!" This sounds pious, but it is not biblical. What this implies is that these other "side" issues regarding the Great Tribulation, the rapture, and the day of the Lore's wrath were not concerns for the biblical writers. It may come as a surprise, however, that the biblical writers themselves did not believe that it was sufficient simply to know that Christ is returning. Indeed, Jesus is coming back, and there is no question that knowing this truth should propel us to holy living. But Jesus himself ominously warns us to be aware of what will happen before he returns: "See, I have told you beforehand" (Matt. 24:25). Jesus, Paul, and the book of Revelation consistently teach that the church will have her faith tested by the Antichrist and his persecution during the great tribulation...that requires the steadfast endurance of the saints.[93]

---

[92] Alan E. Kurchner is a biblical scholar with a Ph.D. in New Testament (McMaster Divinity College); M.A. in Biblical Languages (Gordon-Conwell Theological Seminary); Graduate Studies in New Testament Textual Criticism (Harvard Divinity); and a B.A. in Philosophy (University of Wisconsin-Eau Claire).
[93] Alan E Kurchner, *A Very Short Introduction*, (Pompton Lakes, NJ: Eschatos Publishing, 2014), 2.

The church is filled with different positions when it comes to the rapture and the end of the age. Many have seen the timing of the rapture distorted and relegated to the fringe of Christianity—as long as the believer is "ready" to be raptured, then when it happens is not important. Although I feel that the rapture timing should not be a point of division within the church, I would ask the question, what is meant by "ready"? What exactly does the Bible teach we are to be ready for? There are two basic positions about the timing of the rapture which carry two distinct results concerning readiness: pre-tribulation and post-tribulation. The first holds to the thought that Jesus will come for His church *before* the seventieth week of Daniel begins, thus the church will not experience the time of persecution at the hands of the Antichrist. This time stamp is specifically mentioned by Jesus in the Olivet Discourse, and Jesus refers the listener back to the book of Daniel to understand the timing of this event.[94] The pre-tribulation position holds to the timing of the seven-year tribulation period being a period of the wrath of God, thus the name *pre* (before) *tribulation.* Post-tribulation holds to the idea that the rapture of the saints will not occur until the very end of the tribulation period, traditionally making the sounding of the seventh trumpet to be the "last" trumpet of 1 Corinthians 15:52 and the trumpet of God in 1 Thessalonians 4:16. This position adheres to the idea that the church will be safe within God's wrath and not removed from it. There is one more position that very few hold to but is worth a mention. This position is referred to as

[94] Matt. 24:15 & Dan. 9:27

mid-tribulation. In this view, the church will go through the less severe trouble at the first half of the tribulation period but will be raptured out when the abomination of desolation reveals himself at the midpoint of the seven years, and the Lord will pour out His wrath upon him.

Considering all three positions (considering the mid position as pre-tribulation), the pre and mid positions argue that the church will not experience the wrath of God, which according to Romans 5:9, 1 Thessalonians 1:10, 5:9, and Revelation 3:10 is what the Bible clearly teaches. However, where the pre-tribulation position loses its biblical support is by making the entire seventieth week of Daniel the wrath of God, specifically the intense persecution at the hands of the Antichrist against Jews and what they call tribulation saints. If the Great Tribulation is also the wrath of God, then that position would logically place the persecution and the killing of the people of God on the shoulders of the Father and not the activity of Satan. Post-tribulation maintains that the church will undergo the persecution of the Antichrist as the biblical apocalyptic passages clearly teach. The elect of God will become the targets of his persecution according to the Olivet Discourse (Matthew 24:21-22, 29-31), the letters of Paul (2 Thessalonians 2:1-8), and the revelation of Jesus given to John (Revelation 12:13-17;13:3-10, 14:9-12). But this position, like the pre-tribulation position, has a fatal flaw when it comes to the timing of the rapture. The post view has the rapture occurring at the very end of the seventieth week of Daniel, placing the saints, both dead and alive, meeting Christ in the air and then immediately turning around with Him back to the earth to participate in the battle of Armageddon. This position eliminates the clear biblical teaching that the resurrected and raptured saints are brought to heaven for the Bema Seat of Christ and the Marriage Supper of the Lamb (which Jesus told John would occur in heaven and before the Battle of Armageddon[95]), and it necessitates a rapture that never takes the church into heaven. Although there is agreement on the seventieth week of Daniel, the millennial kingdom, the Day of the Lord's wrath against the wicked, and the battle of Armageddon, the rapture timing purported by pre- and post- tribulation positions are not found anywhere in scripture. The only way one can deduce the timing of the rapture in these positions would be to begin with a presupposition, and then induce that position into scripture.

There is however a rapture timing position that uses all of the clear biblical teaching of both positions, synthesizing and harmonizing all the proof texts together, without any presupposition, around one clearly stated event that has much prophecy attached to it and will be undeniable in its time. It is the sign that Jesus refers to in the Olivet Discourse, the sign that would immediately precede the sign of His coming: the sign of the sun, moon, and stars.[96] This cosmic event involving the sun, moon, and stars being disrupted all at the same time is found in the books of Isaiah, Ezekiel, and Joel directly, and indirectly within other old testament prophetic books. Then, as seen in the New

---

[95] Rev. 19:7
[96] Gen. 1:14-19

Testament books of Mathew, Mark, Luke, Acts and Revelation, it becomes the key to understanding the Day of the Lord and the rescue of the saints. Stated simply: The wrath of God is not the entire seven-year period of Daniel's seventieth week. The first half is referred to as the birth pangs by Jesus separating the seals of Revelation 6 as the pre-wrath conditions on the earth. The Great Tribulation will be the rage of Satan through the persecution of the Antichrist, also known as the abomination that causes desolation. This event is not the wrath of God as the Antichrist is given permission to persecute the Jews and the yet to be raptured church. Jesus tells us that the time of Great Tribulation will be cut short due to the tactical launching of the Day of the Lord marked by the sign in the sun, moon and stars.[97] It is then that the rage of Satan against the elect of God will be immediately terminated by the brightness of the coming of Jesus upon the clouds.[98]

---

[97] Two Old Testament prophets and four New Testament writers confirm the awesome heavenly signs that will be manifested before the Day of the Lord begins (following references in the King James Version): Isaiah 13:6-13 (v.10) "For the stars of heaven and the constellations thereof shall not give their light: the sun shall be darkened in his going forth, and the moon shall not cause her light to shine." Joel 2:31 "The sun shall be turned into darkness, and the moon into blood, before the great and terrible Day of the Lord come." Matthew 24:29 "Immediately after the tribulation of those days shall the sun be darkened, and the moon shall not give her light, and the stars shall fall from heaven, and the powers of the heavens shall be shaken." Mark 13:24-25 "But in those days after that tribulation, the sun shall be darkened, and the moon shall not give her light, And the stars of heaven shall fall, and the powers that are in heaven shall be shaken." Acts 2:20 "The sun shall be turned into darkness, and the moon into blood, before that great and notable Day of the Lord come." Revelation 6:12 "And I beheld when He had opened the sixth seal, and, lo, there was a great earthquake; and the sun became black as sackcloth of hair, and the moon became as blood."

[98] With the world cast into utter darkness, the sign of Christ's coming immediately follows. John describes the return with these words: "Behold, He is coming with the clouds, and every eye will see Him, even those who pierced Him" (Rev. 1:7). The great cloud rider of Daniel 7 will appear in great brightness in the sky just as the

There will be removal of those that are being persecuted from the earth, leaving the wicked remaining who will then experience the wrath of God through the trumpet and the bowl judgments. Thus, the rapture of the church must occur sometime during the Antichrist's persecution (the scriptural post-tribulation position) and before God pours out His wrath (the scriptural pre-tribulation position). Not only that but many of the early church fathers, who wrote of the end-time events, held to the same general premise that the church would undergo persecution at the hand of the Antichrist during the Great Tribulation and then be delivered, as they show in their writings. Hippolytus and Irenaeus are two good examples, the latter of which wrote:

> And therefore, when in the end the Church shall be suddenly caught up from this, it is said, "There shall be tribulation such as has not been since the beginning, neither shall be." For this is the last contest of the righteous, in which, when they overcome they are crowned with incorruption. (Against Heresies, 5.29)[99]

When the scriptural description of the Great Tribulation is embraced by more of the mainstream church, we will have to consider the fact that most of the objections to this position are fear based and fly in the face of American Exceptionalism and economic prosperity as being the solution to the problem. This begs the self analysis of every

---

angels had prophesied at His ascension: "this same Jesus who was taken up from you into heaven, will so come in like manner." Paul states that the lawless one will be destroyed with the brightness of His coming (2 Thess. 2:8).

[99] Alan Fuller, "What view of eschatology did the early church believe?" Stack Exchange, October 9, 2015.

first world believer: Are you putting your confidence in *God's Scripture* or the *world's script*? Is it Christ directing your worldview, or is culture directing your Christ-view? The past couple of years have demonstrated the unrelenting commitment of culture to dictate to our nation (especially the church) how we ought to view society and how it ought to shape the lives of generations. The Bible is viewed as archaic and flawed, and those that follow it as the unadulterated Word of God are seen as mindless bigots. The world is asking religious Americans to soften the message and portray a more tolerant Jesus as culture continues to be formed by social media. It accedes its dictates regardless of the tenets of the Word. The question that we must wrestle with daily is, if the Word contradicts the world or even our own sensibility, where must our loyalty rest? Peter faced this question when considering the words of Jesus in John chapter 6:

> He who eats My flesh and drinks My blood abides in Me, and I in him. As the living Father sent Me, and I live because of the Father, so he who feeds on Me will live because of Me. This is the bread which came down from heaven—not as your fathers ate the manna and are dead. He who eats this bread will live forever." These things He said in the synagogue as He taught in Capernaum. Therefore, many of His disciples, when they heard this, said, "This is a hard saying; who can understand it?" When Jesus knew in Himself that His disciples complained about this, He said to them, "Does this offend you? What then if you

> should see the Son of Man ascend where He was before? It is the Spirit who gives life; the flesh profits nothing. The words that I speak to you are spirit, and they are life. But there are some of you who do not believe." For Jesus knew from the beginning who they were who did not believe, and who would betray Him. And He said, "Therefore I have said to you that no one can come to Me unless it has been granted to him by My Father." From that time many of His disciples went back and walked with Him no more. Then Jesus said to the twelve, "Do you also want to go away?" But Simon Peter answered Him, "Lord, to whom shall we go? You have the words of eternal life. Also, we have come to believe and know that You are the Christ, the Son of the living God." (John 6:56-69)

The 2020 election cycle brought the church to a crossroads in its awareness of its trust level in the Spirit. Although America has been a great tool in the hand of the Lord to bring the gospel to the world, there were always clear lines of division between the kingdom of God and the nation of the United States. America is undoubtedly secular at its founding although it used biblical principles to bring about its distinct freedom and moral dignity of its citizenship. Now there is such an intertwining of the two that people believe the only way to be patriotic is to be Christian and vice versa. This has morphed into the idea of one political party being God's way and the other being Satan's way; the decision of which party is which depends on one's social justice leanings.

I most certainly am proud to be a citizen of the United States of America. I am a student of its history and committed to the American Constitution, which is without doubt the greatest governmental document in the world. I am committed to vote in elections that best assist the desired conditions and principles of the American Constitution according to my moral positions as it pertains to the Word of God. However good this document is and whatever good it has attempted to perpetuate across the centuries, it is <u>not</u> the Word of God and is <u>not</u> divinely inspired. All political parties, all governmental good, every activity of man, including the American Constitution, are products of this present evil age. A politician or a political party can win my vote, but it can never win my devotion. The ultimate devotion of our hearts as believers in Jesus must be to the Word of God alone. We must not judge each other by party affiliation. Our responsibility is to see each other *only* through the cross.

> And I, brethren, when I came to you . . . I determined not to know anything among you except Jesus Christ and Him crucified. (1 Corinthians 2:1-2)

American citizens are drifting further away from biblical foundations. The American Church is in deep division. There has been a resurgence of the idea that persecution might actually be coming.[100] I believe that every pastor needs to consider this as a potential reality. Are we doing what we need to do to prepare the spiritual attitudes and biblical confidence of our congregations in direct accordance with the end-time scriptures?

> Have confidence in your leaders and submit to their authority, because they keep watch over you as those who must give an account. Do this so that their work will be a joy, not a burden, for that would be of no benefit to you. (Heb. 13:17)

Jesus gave us notice after he gave us warnings concerning the times at the end. He made promises that we would have hardship in the world and admonished us to be courageous while we endure it.[101] In Matthew 24, we have the clearest timeline in conjunction with the vision of John in Revelation:

> Therefore when you see the abomination of desolation spoken of by Daniel the prophet, standing in the holy place (whoever reads let him understand) . . . then there will be great tribulation [Gr. *thlipsis*][102] such as has not been since the beginning of the world until this time, no nor ever shall be. And unless those

---

[100] The October Evangelical Leaders Survey asked U.S. evangelical leaders about their experience with persecution and their projections for the future. While only 32 percent indicated that they have been persecuted for their Christian faith, 76 percent expect they will be persecuted in coming years.

[101] John 16:33 "These things I have spoken to you, that in Me you may have peace. In the world you will have tribulation; but be of good cheer, I have overcome the world."

[102] Greek word *thlipsis*: oppression, affliction, tribulation, distress, straits

> days were shortened no flesh would be saved but for the elect's sake those days will be shortened. See I have told you beforehand. (Matthew 24:15-25)

The prevalent teaching of the church being raptured before the beginning of Daniel's 70th week does not align with the biblical scriptures nor the apostolic witness. There is not one explicit scripture that points anyone to the church not experiencing tribulation. On the contrary, Paul makes it very clear that the church will face the antichrist, called the man of sin, before she is raptured.[103] The late John Walvoord of the Dallas Theological Seminary admitted in his book, *The Rapture Question*, that the early church fathers did not subscribe to pre-tribulation thinking. We must understand that the American Church has not been tried in most, if not all, of her history. And as much as we have enjoyed and prospered under this time of peace, we have also grown complacent, which is typical when opposition eludes us. The seven churches of Revelation were all in the prosperous regions of the Roman province at the height of its prosperity. Only two of the seven are given only commendation, and those were the two that were experiencing a degree of suffering, while the two that received the harshest corrections were basking in their riches and prosperity. It is in the times of suffering that the church increases in faith and prayer, and

---

[103] 2 Thes. 2:1-3 "Concerning the coming of our Lord Jesus Christ and our gathering together to Him. . . let no one deceive you for that Day will not come until the man of sin is revealed."

in that, their identity becomes cemented. Dr. Michael Brown, a leader in the Messianic Movement, made this statement:

> In times of suffering, the Church realizes who she is and what she really has to live for. Jesus never promised us non-tribulation; He promised that we would have tribulation in the world and said that we should be courageous because He has already defeated the world. Persecution is the Church's default setting, the setting in which she was born. Once we become followers of Jesus, our lives in this world become forfeit, while we also gain the promise of true life worth living, life that lasts forever.[104]

The American Church needs a reset. This is the only way to complete the process of becoming the glorious, spotless Bride.[105] The idea that the church will go through the Great Tribulation (the rage of Satan) will cause us to wrestle with the question: how do I survive? To me this is the wrong question. The end-time church is not about survival but is about obedience. There are doors of ministry functions that Jesus will open to bring in the final harvest; we already have that confidence before us. Survival is not the objective; the will of God is.[106] Our response to the times of trouble should never be formed around

---

[104] Dr. Michael Brown and Craig Keener, *Not Afraid of the Antichrist: Why We Don't Believe in a Pre-Tribulation Rapture*, (Bloomington MN: Chosen Books 2019), 210.
[105] Eph. 5:27 ". . . and to present her to Himself as a glorious church, without stain or wrinkle or any such blemish, but holy and blameless."
[106] Luke 22:42 "Father, if it is Your will, take this cup away from Me; nevertheless not My will, but Yours, be done."

how to survive the trouble, but how the will of God will be revealed, as a result of the trouble. This will ultimately be the basis for the victorious church. We will only be triumphant within the defense of His will being manifested through us, even if His will is martyrdom. This is still the safest place to be. Consider Revelation 6:9-11:

> When He opened the fifth seal, I saw under the altar the souls of those who had been slain for the word of God and for the testimony which they held. And they cried with a loud voice, saying, "How long, O Lord, holy and true, until You judge and avenge our blood on those who dwell on the earth?" Then a white robe was given to each of them; and it was said to them that they should rest a little while longer, until both the number of their fellow servants and their brethren, who would be killed as they were, was completed.

These martyrs are not those that have been killed throughout church history. They are specific to the time of the Great Tribulation. It is fair to say they have experienced the ultimate tribulation for the sake of the name of Jesus. Amid their crying out for justice they are told to wait until the completion of the number of their fellow martyrs. God has sovereignly determined that a certain number of believers will die during the Great Tribulation. Have these martyrs been defeated? From the point of view of the enemies of God, the answer would be an emphatic *yes*; but if they are fulfilling the requirement and will of God, then the answer is *not at all!* They are victorious . . . as shown in the encouragement of rest and the distribution of the white robes.

The idea of martyrdom and death is not an experience we want to take lightly. We must also understand that at least one of every eight Christians worldwide deal with this issue constantly.[107, 108] Survival is not our biblical goal; doing the will of God and whatever that eventuates is to be our yes-and-amen.[109] It is easy to say yes-and-amen when the promises provide for us honor, glory, riches, and long life. Jesus' last promise to the disciples, just days before their world absolutely fell apart—due to the impending crucifixion of Jesus—was this: "I have told you these things, so that in me you may have peace. In this world you will have tribulation [Gr. *thlipsis*][110] But take heart! I have overcome the world" (John 16:33 ESV).

The church experiencing the Great Tribulation was the prevailing understanding throughout most of church history. This idea has fallen out but is coming back onto the scene in these last days. This has given rise to survival preppers gathering weapons and making bunkers in the woods. Some ministries are selling buckets of food to store in basements in anticipation of the mark of the beast food shortages. Although I am not against people preparing for their natural

---

[107] "World Watch List 2022," Open Doors, 2021. https://www.opendoorsuk.org/persecution/world-watch-list/

[108] 1 of 8 Christians equals 350,000,000 people.

[109] 2 Cor. 1:20 "For all the promises of God in Him are Yes and in Him are Amen, to the glory of God [done] through us."

[110] Greek word *thlipsis*: oppression, affliction, tribulation, distress, straits

needs, that is not what is in sight, nor is it the thing that is needed. The desire to preserve our way of life is a western mindset. We have gotten so comfortable with the things of this world and the beauty of the American way that we have been lulled to sleep, which is contrary to the mindset that we ought to have. Jesus made it clear. He did not say to the churches of Revelation "he who survives" but "he who overcomes."[111]

[111] The term "overcomer" comes from the Greek *nikao*, "to conquer, prevail, triumph, overcome." This verb is found 28 times in 24 verses in the New Testament.

CHAPTER ELEVEN

The Door of Escape

Every believer is an overcomer of the world in the realm of salvation.[112] One just needs to simply believe, and they are victorious over the world. But when it comes to the Great Tribulation, Jesus is not telling us to shut up and take it. Jesus has promised us a way of escape. He said to the church of Philadelphia: "Because you have kept my command to persevere, I also will keep you from the hour of trial which shall come upon the whole world to try those who dwell on the earth" (Revelation 3:10).

Jesus is not saying I will remove you from the trial, but I will protect you within the trial—a way of escape. Part of the overcoming aspect of the end-time church is that the Lord will always give us a way

[112] 1 John 5:5 "Who is it that overcomes the world? Only the one who believes that Jesus is the Son of God."

to do exactly what He is commanding us to do. There is a method to enduring trials. It is done by eliminating the element that makes the trial *trying*, and that element is *the unknown*. Death is the most extreme trial anyone can face, and believers and non-believers handle it in different ways.

> But I do not want you to be ignorant, brethren, concerning those who have fallen asleep, lest you sorrow as others who have no hope. For if we believe that Jesus died and rose again, even so God will bring with Him those who sleep in Jesus. (1 Thessalonians 4:13-14)

We already possess a hope in God about death that is different from the world. If you were facing death right now, and I guaranteed you that you would just fall asleep and awake in heaven, would that take the fear out of death? Most undoubtedly you would answer *yes*. The fear of death for the believer is the fear of the process, not the result. This is where the way of escape comes in:

> Now all these things happened to them as examples, and they were written for our admonition, upon whom the ends of the ages have come. Therefore, let him who thinks he stands take heed lest he fall. No trial has overtaken you except such as is common to man; but God is faithful, who will not allow you to be tested beyond what you are able, but with the trial will also

> make the way of escape, that you may be able to bear it. (1 Corinthians 10:11-13)

> For our momentary, light affliction is producing for us an eternal weight of glory far beyond all comparison. (2 Corinthians 4:17)

Our trials are our way of escape. They are a gift to us; they are the way we train now to be an overcomer at the Great Tribulation. Paul calls our trials "momentary light afflictions" that we are to use to our benefit. Every trial, every tear, every offense, every injustice, every persecution, every death of a loved one, every unexpected sickness, and every financial challenge we should be using to prove our ability in God to be an overcomer.

> Thus, I fight: not as one who beats the air. But I discipline my body and bring it into subjection, lest, when I have preached to others, I myself should become disqualified. (1 Corinthians 9:26-27)

> But we have this treasure in earthen vessels, that the excellence of the power may be of God and not of us. We are hard-pressed on every side, yet not crushed; we are perplexed, but not in despair; persecuted, but not forsaken; struck down, but not destroyed— always carrying about in the body the dying of the Lord Jesus, that the life of Jesus also may be manifested in our body. For we who live are always delivered to death for Jesus' sake, that the life of Jesus also may be manifested in our mortal

> flesh. So then death is working in us, but life in you. (2 Corinthians 4:7-12)

> Many are the afflictions of the righteous one, and Lord Jehovah delivers him from all of them. And he will keep all his bones that not one of them will be broken. (Psalm 34:19-20, ARA)

Every passage of scripture that encourages the church in trials, tribulations, perseverance, and patience are all to be used for end-time strength. In the book of Acts, we are given a narrative of Paul's missionary trips in Iconium and Lystra. It is during the trip to Lystra that we find a peculiar passage that often goes overlooked, due to its strange implication, but comes into perfect view when applied to the opened doors of the Great Tribulation.

> Then Jews from Antioch and Iconium came there; and having persuaded the multitudes, they stoned Paul and dragged him out of the city, supposing him to be dead. However, when the disciples gathered around him, he rose up and went into the city. And the next day he departed with Barnabas to Derbe. And when they had preached the gospel to that city and made many disciples, they returned to Lystra, Iconium, and Antioch, strengthening the souls of the disciples, exhorting them to continue in the faith, and saying, "We must through many tribulations enter the kingdom of God." (Acts 14:19-22)

The first part that is conspicuously absent is the detail from Luke about the medical condition of Paul. One would think that Luke would give much more detail to the stoning of Paul, but there is nothing. At the end of the violence, they suppose Paul to be dead. Though by the time he is out of the city, he seems to have miraculously recovered. I would not be surprised if we begin to hear these types of stories coming out of Afghanistan due to the degree of persecution the church there is facing.

The second unusual part of this passage lies within the last sentence: "Strengthening the souls of the disciples, exhorting them to continue in the faith and saying, 'We must through many tribulations enter the kingdom of God.'" I consider this the title page of the end-times overcomers of the church. There is a message that will strengthen the disciples of Jesus to continue in faith in the midst of persecutions when they will need it the most. "It is in trials that we enter the kingdom." It is through many tribulations (thlipsis) that we must enter the kingdom of God…through the door of escape. The door of escape is found in the motivations of our faith. For the joy set before Him, Jesus endured the cross, despising its shame compared to the result.[113] The writer of Hebrews tells us to fix our eyes on this example, as He is the author and finisher of our faith. Jesus has set up this process, and He will finish it. Jesus is opening the door of escape for

---

[113] Heb. 12:2 ". . . fixing our eyes on Jesus, the pioneer and perfecter of faith. For the joy set before him he endured the cross, scorning its shame, and sat down at the right hand of the throne of God."

those who are going through the end-time tribulation, trained by their own tribulations throughout their lives. During the time of Satan's rage there will be a way of escape. I challenge you to read this end-time passage and be aware of your heart as the Holy Spirit strengthens you through these words:

> So now there is no condemnation for those who belong to Christ Jesus. And because you belong to him, the power of the life-giving Spirit has freed you from the power of sin that leads to death. The law of Moses was unable to save us because of the weakness of our sinful nature. So, God did what the law could not do. He sent his own Son in a body like the bodies we sinners have. And in that body God declared an end to sin's control over us by giving his Son as a sacrifice for our sins. He did this so that the just requirement of the law would be fully satisfied for us, who no longer follow our sinful nature but instead follow the Spirit. Those who are dominated by the sinful nature think about sinful things, but those who are controlled by the Holy Spirit think about things that please the Spirit. So, letting your sinful nature control your mind leads to death. But letting the Spirit control your mind leads to life and peace. For the sinful nature is always hostile to God. It never did obey God's laws, and it never will. That's why those who are still under the control of their sinful nature can never please God. But you are not controlled by your sinful nature. You are controlled by the Spirit

if you have the Spirit of God living in you. (And remember that those who do not have the Spirit of Christ living in them do not belong to him at all.) And Christ lives within you, so even though your body will die because of sin, the Spirit gives you life because you have been made right with God. The Spirit of God, who raised Jesus from the dead, lives in you. And just as God raised Christ Jesus from the dead, he will give life to your mortal bodies by this same Spirit living within you. Therefore, dear brothers and sisters, you have no obligation to do what your sinful nature urges you to do. For if you live by its dictates, you will die. But if through the power of the Spirit you put to death the deeds of your sinful nature, you will live. For all who are led by the Spirit of God are children of God. So, you have not received a spirit that makes you fearful slaves. Instead, you received God's Spirit when he adopted you as his own children. Now we call him, "Abba, Father" for his Spirit joins with our spirit to affirm that we are God's children. And since we are his children, we are his heirs. In fact, together with Christ we are heirs of God's glory. But if we are to share his glory, we must also share his suffering. Yet what we suffer now is nothing compared to the glory he will reveal to us later. For all creation is waiting eagerly for that future day when God will reveal who his children really are. Against its will, all creation was subjected to God's curse. But with eager hope, the creation looks forward to the day when it will join God's children in glorious freedom from death and decay. For we know that all creation has been groaning as in the pains of childbirth right up to the present time. And we believers also groan, even though we have the Holy Spirit within us as a foretaste of future glory, for we long for our bodies to be released from sin and suffering. We, too, wait with eager hope for the day when God will give us our full rights as his adopted children, including the new bodies he has promised us. We were given this hope when we were saved. (If we already have something, we don't need to hope for it. But if we look forward to something we don't yet have, we must wait patiently and confidently.) And the Holy Spirit helps us in our weakness. For example, we don't know what God wants us to pray for. But the Holy Spirit prays for us with groanings that cannot be expressed in words. And the Father who knows all hearts knows what the Spirit is saying, for the Spirit pleads for us believers in harmony with God's own will. And we know that God causes everything to work together for the good of those who love God and are called according to his purpose for them. For God knew his people in advance, and he chose them to become like his Son, so that his Son would be the firstborn among many brothers and sisters. And having chosen them, he called them to come to him. And having called them, he gave them right standing with himself. And having given them right standing, he gave them his glory. What shall we say about such wonderful things as these? If God is for us, who can

> ever be against us? Since he did not spare even his own Son but gave him up for us all, won't he also give us everything else? Who dares accuse us whom God has chosen for his own? No one—for God himself has given us right standing with himself. Who then will condemn us? No one—for Christ Jesus died for us and was raised to life for us, and he is sitting in the place of honor at God's right hand, pleading for us. Can anything ever separate us from Christ's love? Does it mean he no longer loves us if we have trouble or calamity, or are persecuted, or hungry, or destitute, or in danger, or threatened with death? (As the Scriptures say, "For your sake we are killed every day; we are being slaughtered like sheep.") No, despite all these things, overwhelming victory is ours through Christ, who loved us. And I am convinced that nothing can ever separate us from God's love. Neither death nor life, neither angels nor demons, neither our fears for today nor our worries about tomorrow—not even the powers of hell can separate us from God's love. No power in the sky above or in the earth below—indeed, nothing in all creation will ever be able to separate us from the love of God that is revealed in Christ Jesus our Lord. (Romans 8 NLT)

There are three objectives to our lives when we finally see Him. The first is exaltation; if we are faithful in the little, then we are trusted with the more in the Millennial kingdom.[114] The second is that we will

---

[114] Luke 16:10: "He that is faithful in a very little is faithful also in much: and he that is unrighteous in a very little is unrighteous also in much."

be given rewards.[115] And finally, the most impressive, the most impactful, and the greatest of all three will be the verbal acclamation from God Himself. How incredible will it be when we hear in person from the one who spoke all of creation into existence;[116] from the one whose voice is as the sound of many waters;[117] the voice of power and majesty, that breaks the cedars of Lebanon;[118] the voice that melts the earth;[119] the voice of thunder;[120] and the voice of heaven saying in the most heartfelt and compassionate tones, "Well done my good and faithful servant, enter into your rest."

There are no conditions attached to our salvation and there is no work that we can perform that would be equal to that gift. Being an overcomer of the end-time church has everything to do with His pleasure and our rewards from Him. Jesus said He will never leave us, even unto the end of the age. He is always with us in divine partnership. There is no clearer demonstration in scripture of this partnership than the prayer of Jesus in John 17:

> "My prayer is not for the world, but for those you have given me, because they belong to you. All who are mine belong to

---

[115] Rev. 22:12 "Behold, I am coming quickly, and My reward is with Me, to render to every man according to what he has done."
[116] Gen. 1:3 "Then God said . . ."
[117] Ezk. 43:2 "And His voice was like the sound of many waters."
[118] Ps. 29:3-9 "The voice of the Lord is powerful, the voice of the Lord is majestic, the voice of the Lord breaks the cedars of Lebanon."
[119] Ps. 46:6 "He raised His voice, the earth melted."
[120] Ps. 18:13. "The Lord also thundered in the heavens, and the Most High uttered His voice."

you, and you have given them to me, so they bring me glory. Now I am departing from the world; they are staying in this world, but I am coming to you. Holy Father, you have given me your name; now protect them by the power of your name so that they will be united just as we are. During my time here, I protected them by the power of the name you gave me. I guarded them so that not one was lost, except the one headed for destruction, as the Scriptures foretold. Now I am coming to you. I told them many things while I was with them in this world so they would be filled with my joy. I have given them your word. And the world hates them because they do not belong to the world, just as I do not belong to the world. I'm not asking you to take them out of the world, but to keep them safe from the evil one. They do not belong to this world any more than I do. Make them holy by your truth; teach them your word, which is truth. Just as you sent me into the world, I am sending them into the world. And I give myself as a holy sacrifice for them so they can be made holy by your truth. I am praying not only for these disciples but also for all who will ever believe in me through their message. I pray that they will all be one, just as you and I are one—as you are in me, Father, and I am in you. And may they be in us so that the world will believe you sent me. I have given them the glory you gave me, so they may be one as we are one. I am in them and you are in me. May they experience such perfect unity that the world will know that you sent me and that

> you love them as much as you love me. Father, I want these whom you have given me to be with me where I am. Then they can see all the glory you gave me because you loved me even before the world began! O righteous Father, the world doesn't know you, but I do; and these disciples know you sent me. I have revealed you to them, and I will continue to do so. Then your love for me will be in them, and I will be in them." (John 17:9-26 NLT)

We are not encouraged to hasten the day of persecution, or pray for persecution; on the contrary, the Bible instructs us to pray to live a life peaceably in godliness and reverence as a means for people to come to the knowledge of the truth.[121] This is not in opposition to persecution but despite it. We must know the plan of God concerning the end times and our role in it, so we are not caught off guard like the rest of the world (1 Thessalonians 5:1-10). It will be through our confidence and trust in the Lord during the times of trouble that the Lord will be glorified by our light shining in the darkness. The world will see our good works in the light we produce through the Holy Spirit now, in the challenges ahead, and unto His return.

---

[121] 1 Tim. 2:1-4 "Therefore I exhort first of all that supplications, prayers, intercessions, and giving of thanks be made for all men . . . we may lead a quiet and peaceable life in all godliness and reverence. For this is good and acceptable in the sight of God our Savior, who desires all men to be saved and to come to the knowledge of the truth."

But concerning the times and the seasons, brethren, you have no need that I should write to you. For you yourselves know perfectly that the day of the Lord so comes as a thief in the night. For when they say, "Peace and safety!" then sudden destruction comes upon them, as labor pains upon a pregnant woman. And they shall not escape. But you, brethren, are not in darkness, so that this Day should overtake you as a thief. You are all sons of light and sons of the day. We are not of the night nor of darkness. Therefore let us not sleep, as others do, but let us watch and be sober. For those who sleep, sleep at night, and those who get drunk are drunk at night. But let us who are of the day be sober, putting on the breastplate of faith and love, and as a helmet the hope of salvation. For God did not appoint us to wrath, but to obtain salvation through our Lord Jesus Christ, who died for us, that whether we wake or sleep, we should live together with Him. Therefore comfort each other and edify one another, just as you also are doing. (1 Thessalonians 5:1-10)

CONCLUSION

> That I may know Him and the power of His resurrection, and the fellowship of His sufferings, being conformed to His death, if, by any means, I may attain to the resurrection from the dead. (Philippians 3:10-11)

We live in a country where the power of the evil one to persecute the church has been quelled because of the covenants and prayerful agreements made by many of the founders of our rich heritage in America. On April 29th of 1607, a new nation was born at Cape Henry, Virginia. One hundred souls traveled from England and landed at the southern entrance to the Chesapeake Bay. There they erected a seven-foot wooden cross and consecrated this nation to the glory of God. The Reverend Robert Hunt was given the task of overseeing the spiritual needs of settlers and promoting the conversion of American Indians of the region. Upon arrival, after giving thanks for their long passage, he declared, "From these very shores, the gospel shall go forth to not only this New World, but the entire world."[122] At the signing of the Declaration of Independence in Philadelphia on July 5th of 1776, Samuel Adams stood to proclaim, "We have this day restored the sovereign. To Him alone men ought to be obedient. He reigns in heaven and from the rising to the setting sun, may His Kingdom Come."[123]

These are just two small examples of hundreds of declarations that have been made within the founding documents of not only our nation but many of the townships and cities that dot America. New Jersey (my home state) is saturated with signs and markers that commemorate and memorialize the rich colonial heritage of the New World pursuing a "more perfect union" steeped within the Christian model and the propagation of the teachings of Jesus Christ. According to Lloyd Turner's book, *Highways of Holiness*, there are fourteen "wells of revival" that lie alongside New Jersey's twenty-eight-mile stretch of Interstate 78 connecting Pennsylvania to New York City. It

---

[122] "The Reverend Robert Hunt," Jamestown Rediscovery: Historic Jamestowne, accessed August, 2021, https://historicjamestowne.org/archaeology/chancel-burials/founders/robert-hunt/
[123] William J. Federer, *America's God and Country Encyclopedia of Quotations*, (St. Louis, MO: Amerisearch Inc, 1994), 143.

begins with the home of David Brainard and his missionary call in 1744 in Martins Creek, PA, and ends with Jeremiah Lanphier's Fulton Street Prayer Meeting Revival of 1857-58.[124] These markers are reminders to us that there is an underlying covenant with God made by those that established the foundation of this country and the establishment of its communities. Although man may have forgotten the meaning and sentiments behind these declarations and covenants, God still remembers and honors them in spite of the forgetfulness and disregard of subsequent generations.

The year was 1630 when the ship *Arbella* was en route to the Massachusetts Bay Colony as Puritan leader John Winthrop penned and delivered his sermon, "A Model of Christian Charity," to the people that would become a new nation. The sermon and its words were known and preserved throughout the colonization and the American Revolution, and they were reintroduced by President Ronald Reagan and many presidents after him with the phrase, "America is a city upon a hill." This is what most consider the foundational sermon of America. In it he sets down the precepts needed for there to be a community that can survive the evils of the natural world and the "two rules whereby we are to walk one towards another: Justice and Mercy." As Winthrop called people to commit themselves to brotherly love and unity as the way of success for the American colony, he ends his sermon with the words borrowed from Moses in Deuteronomy 30:15-18, inserting what

---

[124] Lloyd Turner, *Highway of Holiness:Preparing the Way for the Lord*, (Self-pub., CreateSpace, 2006), 189.

he understands to be the contemporary application of the consequences for pursuing other interests rather than God. Winthrop writes:

> We shall find that the God of Israel is among us, when ten of us shall be able to resist a thousand of our enemies; when he shall make us a praise and glory that men shall say of succeeding plantations, "the Lord make it likely that of New England." For we must consider that we shall be as a city upon a hill. The eyes of all people are upon us. So that if we shall deal falsely with our God in this work we have undertaken, and so cause him to withdraw his present help from us, we shall be made a story and a by-word through the world. We shall open the mouths of enemies to speak evil of the ways of God, and all professors for God's sake. We shall shame the faces of many of God's worthy servants and cause their prayers to be turned into curses upon us till we be consumed out of the good land whither we are going.
>
> I shall shut up this discourse with that exhortation of Moses, that faithful servant of the Lord, in his last farewell to Israel, Deut. 30: Beloved there is now set before us life and good, Death and evil, in that we are commanded this day to love the Lord our God, and to love one another, to walk in his ways and to keep his Commandments and his Ordinance and his laws, and the articles of our Covenant with him, that we may live and be multiplied, and that the Lord our God may bless us in the land

> whither we go to possess it. But if our hearts shall turn away, so that we will not obey, but shall be seduced, and worship and serve other gods, our pleasure and profits, and serve them; it is propounded unto us this day, we shall surely perish out of the good land whither we pass over this vast sea to possess it. Therefore let us choose life—that we, and our seed may live, by obeying His voice and cleaving to Him, for He is our life and our prosperity.[125]

The passage of Deuteronomy 30 that Winthrop quotes is the message of Moses as the Hebrews were about to enter into the Promised Land. It is clear that Winthrop saw the New World as significant as the Holy Land and that the establishment of the colony must maintain the covenants and commands of the God of Israel and thus become *the city upon a hill*, bringing the gospel of Jesus to the world. It is for this reason that I believe the American Church has endured thus far and will continue to be the shining city on a hill only as long as she maintains her position and commitment to the scriptures. However, this will not exempt us from persecution that the whole world will face, but instead, it will strengthen us to remain faithful to the end.

The end-time open doors of the end of the age will be the sustaining force and the enduring confidence for the church worldwide. It will be a time when God will honor all covenants and declarations as

---

[125] This quote includes a slight modernization of spelling for clarity. For original text, see: https://history.hanover.edu/texts/winthmod.html.

He transitions the kingdoms of this world into the kingdoms of our God and of His Christ. The coming persecution is a time for us to be in the right position with the proper amount of strength and confidence so we will be ready for "the revealing of the sons of God" in the last days.

> For I consider that the sufferings of this present time are not worthy to be compared with the glory which shall be revealed in us. For the earnest expectation of the creation eagerly waits for the revealing of the sons of God. For the creation was subjected to futility, not willingly, but because of Him who subjected it in hope; because the creation itself also will be delivered from the bondage of corruption into the glorious liberty of the children of God. For we know that the whole creation groans and labors with birth pangs together until now. (Romans 8:18-22)

There are many countries on the earth where martyrdom and persecution are the makeup of normal Christianity. There are hundreds of thousands of people that have come to faith under the threat of torture, and even death, as opposed to honor, glory, and prosperity. These are those who do not attend a crusade to hear the latest worship concert and a feel-good message. They are instead drawn by the Holy Spirit to hear the gospel, usually in whispers, and then through the gift of grace through faith given by God, they place themselves and their family in harm's way to align themselves with the lover of their soul. The open doors of Revelation 3 have already been open for them as they continue to gather under the threat of death to pray night and day, to share the gospel, and to dwell in prophetic unction with confidence of not loving their lives even unto death. The American Church must find a way to come into fellowship with the reality of Christ's sufferings through these persecuted churches as a way of developing within herself how she can cultivate confidence to endure. One way that my home church has begun to fellowship with the sufferings of our brethren is by partaking of communion together every Sunday at the beginning of the service. When we consider the sufferings of Jesus through the bread, we take a moment to highlight a specific region of persecuted believers and pray for them. In doing so, we are seeing a renewed appreciation for our salvation as well as the confidence through the endurance of our brothers and sisters around the globe.[126] This is just one way that we can begin recognizing and building our stamina for the coming crisis. However, persecution is not only for some far away land but must be considered by everyone that claims the name of Jesus. Christianity is the only religion whose main leader, who we are called to follow by taking up our own torture device, died a martyr's death at the hands of those in his own household. It does not make for a popular website or conference advertisement, but it is what many of the Christian population of China, Pakistan, India, and Afghanistan must consider daily, and was the case for the first three-hundred years of Christian history. How did it survive? Jesus said that He is holding open a door that no man can shut. The Bible is clear

---

[126] Some helpful websites: www.persecution.com; opendoorsusa.org; catalyticministires.com

that these last days and the last generation just before the return of Jesus will be marked by severe persecution and martyrdom, but it will also be answered by the greatest unity and Holy Spirit power ever witnessed in any generation.

> And it shall come to pass afterward, that I will pour out My Spirit on all flesh; your sons and your daughters shall prophesy, your old men shall dream dreams, your young men shall see visions. And also on My menservants and on My maidservants I will pour out My Spirit in those days. And I will show wonders in the heavens and in the earth. (Joel 2:28-30 KJV)
>
> But Peter, standing up with the eleven, raised his voice and said to them, "Men of Judea and all who dwell in Jerusalem, let this be known to you, and heed my words. For these are not drunk, as you suppose, since it is only the third hour of the day. But this is what was spoken by the prophet Joel: 'And it shall come to pass in the last days, says God, that I will pour out of My Spirit on all flesh; your sons and your daughters shall prophesy, your young men shall see visions, your old men shall dream dreams. And on My menservants and on My maidservants I will pour out My Spirit in those days; and they shall prophesy. I will show wonders in heaven above and signs in the earth beneath.'" (Acts 2:14-19)

During the darkest hour of the crisis, God's people will shine brightest because they have been preparing themselves, making themselves ready through the storm, and will be victorious in love unto the return of the King. The church's preparation will not come as a result of the will of man but with the direct intervention of the Holy Spirit and the unity of the Bride pursuing Jesus in the face of trouble.

I believe that the end-time church will need the confidence in knowing that Jesus is partnering with us, that He has been aware of and has planned for these days way ahead of us. The divine strategy of the open doors combined with the end-time outpouring of the Holy Spirit within a confident and lovesick church will be the combination that will bring many into the kingdom and the victory of the Bride. In those last days, the church will be functioning at its highest anointing against the onslaught of the devil through his emissaries. And then, just when the crisis is at its darkest—every eye will see Him, and the sky will be broken by the brightness of His coming. His shout will bring the universe to attention, and the entire earth will know on that Day the awesome power and majesty of the One who opens the door that no one can ever shut!

> The Lord is my light and my salvation; whom shall I fear? The Lord is the strength of my life; of whom shall I be afraid? When the wicked came against me to eat up my flesh, my enemies and foes, they stumbled and fell. Though an army may encamp against me, my heart shall not fear; though war may rise against me, in this I will be confident. One thing I have desired of the Lord, that I will seek: That I may dwell in the house of the Lord

all the days of my life, to behold the beauty of the Lord, and to inquire in His temple. (Psalm 27:1-4)